Valuation Advisory
Complete Self-Assessment Guide

D1796552

The guidance in this Self-Assessment is based on Valuation Advisory best practices and standards in business process architecture, design and quality management. The guidance is also based on the professional judgment of the individual collaborators listed in the Acknowledgments.

Notice of rights

Trademarks

Table of Contents

About The Art of Service

The Art of Service, Business Process Architects since 2000, is dedicated to helping stakeholders achieve excellence.

Defining, designing, creating, and implementing a process to solve a stakeholders challenge or meet an objective is the most valuable role… In EVERY group, company, organization and department.

Unless you're talking a one-time, single-use project, there should be a process. Whether that process is managed and implemented by humans, AI, or a combination of the two, it needs to be designed by someone with a complex enough perspective to ask the right questions.

Someone capable of asking the right questions and step back and say, 'What are we really trying to accomplish here? And is there a different way to look at it?'

With The Art of Service's Standard Requirements Self-Assessments, we empower people who can do just that — whether their title is marketer, entrepreneur, manager, salesperson, consultant, Business Process Manager, executive assistant, IT Manager, CIO etc... —they are the people who rule the future. They are people who watch the process as it happens, and ask the right questions to make the process work better.

Contact us when you need any support with this Self-Assessment and any help with templates, blue-prints and examples of standard documents you might need:

http://theartofservice.com
service@theartofservice.com

Acknowledgments

This checklist was developed under the auspices of The Art of Service, chaired by Gerardus Blokdyk.

Representatives from several client companies participated in the preparation of this Self-Assessment.

In addition, we are thankful for the design and printing services provided.

Included Resources - how to access

Included with your purchase of the book is the Valuation Advisory Self-Assessment Spreadsheet Dashboard which contains all questions and Self-Assessment areas and auto-generates insights, graphs, and project RACI planning - all with examples to get you started right away.

How? Simply send an email to
access@theartofservice.com
with this books' title in the subject to get the Valuation Advisory Self Assessment Tool right away.

You will receive the following contents with New and Updated specific criteria:

- The latest quick edition of the book in PDF

- The latest complete edition of the book in PDF, which criteria correspond to the criteria in...

- The Self-Assessment Excel Dashboard, and...

- Example pre-filled Self-Assessment Excel Dashboard to get familiar with results generation

- In-depth specific Checklists covering the topic

- Project management checklists and templates to assist with implementation

INCLUDES LIFETIME SELF ASSESSMENT UPDATES

Every self assessment comes with Lifetime Updates and Lifetime Free Updated Books. Lifetime Updates is an industry-first feature which allows you to receive verified self assessment updates, ensuring you always have the most accurate information at your fingertips.

Get it now- you will be glad you did - do it now, before you forget.

Send an email to **access@theartofservice.com** with this books' title in the subject to get the Valuation Advisory Self Assessment Tool right away.

Your feedback is invaluable to us

If you recently bought this book, we would love to hear from you! You can do this by writing a review on amazon (or the online store where you purchased this book) about your last purchase! As part of our continual service improvement process, we love to hear real client experiences and feedback.

How does it work?
To post a review on Amazon, just log in to your account and click on the Create Your Own Review button (under Customer Reviews) of the relevant product page. You can find examples of product reviews in Amazon. If you purchased from another online store, simply follow their procedures.

What happens when I submit my review?
Once you have submitted your review, send us an email at review@theartofservice.com with the link to your review so we can properly thank you for your feedback.

Purpose of this Self-Assessment

This Self-Assessment has been developed to improve understanding of the requirements and elements of Valuation Advisory, based on best practices and standards in business process architecture, design and quality management.

It is designed to allow for a rapid Self-Assessment to determine how closely existing management practices and procedures correspond to the elements of the Self-Assessment.

The criteria of requirements and elements of Valuation Advisory have been rephrased in the format of a Self-Assessment questionnaire, with a seven-criterion scoring system, as explained in this document.

In this format, even with limited background knowledge of

Valuation Advisory, a manager can quickly review existing operations to determine how they measure up to the standards. This in turn can serve as the starting point of a 'gap analysis' to identify management tools or system elements that might usefully be implemented in the organization to help improve overall performance.

How to use the Self-Assessment

On the following pages are a series of questions to identify to what extent your Valuation Advisory initiative is complete in comparison to the requirements set in standards.

To facilitate answering the questions, there is a space in front of each question to enter a score on a scale of '1' to '5'.

1 Strongly Disagree

2 Disagree

3 Neutral

4 Agree

5 Strongly Agree

Read the question and rate it with the following in front of mind:

'In my belief,
the answer to this question is clearly defined'.

There are two ways in which you can choose to interpret this statement;
1. how aware are you that the answer to the question is clearly defined
2. for more in-depth analysis you can choose to gather

evidence and confirm the answer to the question. This obviously will take more time, most Self-Assessment users opt for the first way to interpret the question and dig deeper later on based on the outcome of the overall Self-Assessment.

A score of '1' would mean that the answer is not clear at all, where a '5' would mean the answer is crystal clear and defined. Leave emtpy when the question is not applicable or you don't want to answer it, you can skip it without affecting your score. Write your score in the space provided.

After you have responded to all the appropriate statements in each section, compute your average score for that section, using the formula provided, and round to the nearest tenth. Then transfer to the corresponding spoke in the Valuation Advisory Scorecard on the second next page of the Self-Assessment.

Your completed Valuation Advisory Scorecard will give you a clear presentation of which Valuation Advisory areas need attention.

Valuation Advisory Scorecard Example

Example of how the finalized Scorecard can look like:

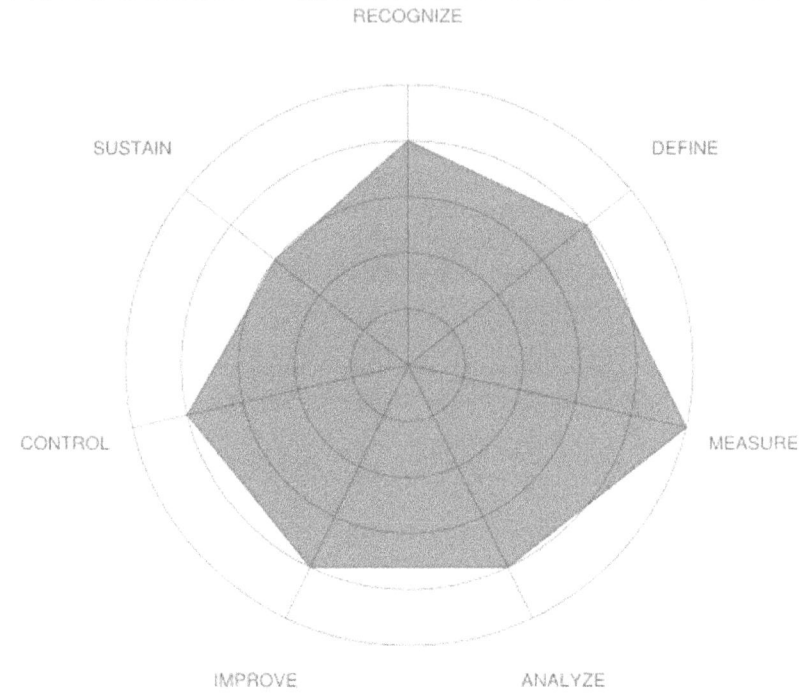

Valuation Advisory Scorecard

Your Scores:

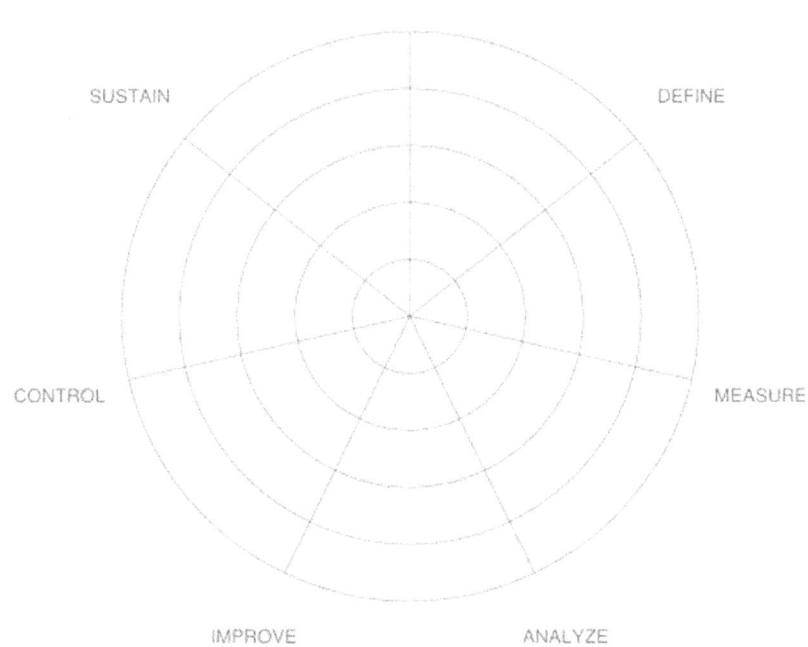

BEGINNING OF THE SELF-ASSESSMENT:

CRITERION #1: RECOGNIZE

INTENT: Be aware of the need for change. Recognize that there is an unfavorable variation, problem or symptom.

In my belief, the answer to this question is clearly defined:

5 Strongly Agree

4 Agree

3 Neutral

2 Disagree

1 Strongly Disagree

1. Is it clear when you think of the day ahead of you what activities and tasks you need to complete?
<--- Score

2. What tools and technologies are needed for a custom Valuation Advisory project?
<--- Score

3. What else needs to be measured?

<--- Score

4. Do you have/need 24-hour access to key personnel?
<--- Score

5. As a sponsor, customer or management, how important is it to meet goals, objectives?
<--- Score

6. What does Valuation Advisory success mean to the stakeholders?
<--- Score

7. How are you going to measure success?
<--- Score

8. What should be considered when identifying available resources, constraints, and deadlines?
<--- Score

9. Should you invest in industry-recognized qualications?
<--- Score

10. To what extent does each concerned units management team recognize Valuation Advisory as an effective investment?
<--- Score

11. What information do users need?
<--- Score

12. Have you identified your Valuation Advisory key performance indicators?
<--- Score

13. Who defines the rules in relation to any given issue?
<--- Score

14. What would happen if Valuation Advisory weren't done?
<--- Score

15. What do you need to start doing?
<--- Score

16. What problems are you facing and how do you consider Valuation Advisory will circumvent those obstacles?
<--- Score

17. Who needs to know about Valuation Advisory?
<--- Score

18. Are there any specific expectations or concerns about the Valuation Advisory team, Valuation Advisory itself?
<--- Score

19. Are employees recognized or rewarded for performance that demonstrates the highest levels of integrity?
<--- Score

20. When a Valuation Advisory manager recognizes a problem, what options are available?
<--- Score

21. How are the Valuation Advisory's objectives aligned to the organization's overall business strategy?

<--- Score

22. What are the business objectives to be achieved with Valuation Advisory?
<--- Score

23. What situation(s) led to this Valuation Advisory Self Assessment?
<--- Score

24. Will Valuation Advisory deliverables need to be tested and, if so, by whom?
<--- Score

25. What is the smallest subset of the problem you can usefully solve?
<--- Score

26. Is the need for organizational change recognized?
<--- Score

27. Looking at each person individually – does every one have the qualities which are needed to work in this group?
<--- Score

28. Are your goals realistic? Do you need to redefine your problem? Perhaps the problem has changed or maybe you have reached your goal and need to set a new one?
<--- Score

29. Who else hopes to benefit from it?
<--- Score

30. What are the timeframes required to resolve each

of the issues/problems?
<--- Score

31. Do you need to avoid or amend any Valuation Advisory activities?
<--- Score

32. What activities does the governance board need to consider?
<--- Score

33. Think about the people you identified for your Valuation Advisory project and the project responsibilities you would assign to them. what kind of training do you think they would need to perform these responsibilities effectively?
<--- Score

34. What are your needs in relation to Valuation Advisory skills, labor, equipment, and markets?
<--- Score

35. Will new equipment/products be required to facilitate Valuation Advisory delivery, for example is new software needed?
<--- Score

36. What are the minority interests and what amount of minority interests can be recognized?
<--- Score

37. How does it fit into your organizational needs and tasks?
<--- Score

38. Are there Valuation Advisory problems defined?

<--- Score

39. How do you assess your Valuation Advisory workforce capability and capacity needs, including skills, competencies, and staffing levels?
<--- Score

40. Who had the original idea?
<--- Score

41. How much are sponsors, customers, partners, stakeholders involved in Valuation Advisory? In other words, what are the risks, if Valuation Advisory does not deliver successfully?
<--- Score

42. Are there recognized Valuation Advisory problems?
<--- Score

43. Does Valuation Advisory create potential expectations in other areas that need to be recognized and considered?
<--- Score

44. How do you take a forward-looking perspective in identifying Valuation Advisory research related to market response and models?
<--- Score

45. What prevents you from making the changes you know will make you a more effective Valuation Advisory leader?
<--- Score

46. How can auditing be a preventative security

measure?

<--- Score

47. What are the expected benefits of Valuation Advisory to the business?

<--- Score

48. Do you need different information or graphics?

<--- Score

49. What needs to be done?

<--- Score

50. Consider your own Valuation Advisory project, what types of organizational problems do you think might be causing or affecting your problem, based on the work done so far?

<--- Score

51. What is the problem or issue?

<--- Score

52. Are problem definition and motivation clearly presented?

<--- Score

53. What vendors make products that address the Valuation Advisory needs?

<--- Score

54. For your Valuation Advisory project, identify and describe the business environment, is there more than one layer to the business environment?

<--- Score

55. Do you know what you need to know about

Valuation Advisory?
<--- Score

Add up total points for this section:
_____ = Total points for this section

Divided by: _____ (number of
statements answered) = _____
Average score for this section

Transfer your score to the Valuation
Advisory Index at the beginning of the
Self-Assessment.

CRITERION #2: DEFINE:

INTENT: Formulate the business problem. Define the problem, needs and objectives.

In my belief, the answer to this question is clearly defined:

5 Strongly Agree

4 Agree

3 Neutral

2 Disagree

1 Strongly Disagree

1. Has everyone on the team, including the team leaders, been properly trained?
<--- Score

2. How and when will the baselines be defined?
<--- Score

3. Is there a completed SIPOC representation, describing the Suppliers, Inputs, Process, Outputs, and

Customers?

<--- Score

4. Are approval levels defined for contracts and supplements to contracts?

<--- Score

5. Will team members regularly document their Valuation Advisory work?

<--- Score

6. What was the context?

<--- Score

7. How does the Valuation Advisory manager ensure against scope creep?

<--- Score

8. How would you define the culture at your organization, how susceptible is it to Valuation Advisory changes?

<--- Score

9. What constraints exist that might impact the team?

<--- Score

10. Do the problem and goal statements meet the SMART criteria (specific, measurable, attainable, relevant, and time-bound)?

<--- Score

11. What are the tasks and definitions?

<--- Score

12. What is out of scope?

<--- Score

13. How would you define Valuation Advisory leadership?
<--- Score

14. When are meeting minutes sent out? Who is on the distribution list?
<--- Score

15. Is the current 'as is' process being followed? If not, what are the discrepancies?
<--- Score

16. When was the Valuation Advisory start date?
<--- Score

17. You may have created your quality measures at a time when you lacked resources, technology wasn't up to the required standard, or low service levels were the industry norm. Have those circumstances changed?
<--- Score

18. What is in scope?
<--- Score

19. Does the scope remain the same?
<--- Score

20. Who defines (or who defined) the rules and roles?
<--- Score

21. Is Valuation Advisory currently on schedule according to the plan?
<--- Score

22. Are improvement team members fully trained on Valuation Advisory?
<--- Score

23. What scope do you want your strategy to cover?
<--- Score

24. Are customers identified and high impact areas defined?
<--- Score

25. Is the team formed and are team leaders (Coaches and Management Leads) assigned?
<--- Score

26. What are the Roles and Responsibilities for each team member and its leadership? Where is this documented?
<--- Score

27. Are roles and responsibilities formally defined?
<--- Score

28. What is the scope of the Valuation Advisory effort?
<--- Score

29. How is the team tracking and documenting its work?
<--- Score

30. Are customer(s) identified and segmented according to their different needs and requirements?
<--- Score

31. Is it clearly defined in and to your organization what you do?

<--- Score

32. Has/have the customer(s) been identified?
<--- Score

33. Is there a critical path to deliver Valuation Advisory results?
<--- Score

34. What customer feedback methods were used to solicit their input?
<--- Score

35. Who are the Valuation Advisory improvement team members, including Management Leads and Coaches?
<--- Score

36. What are the boundaries of the scope? What is in bounds and what is not? What is the start point? What is the stop point?
<--- Score

37. How did the Valuation Advisory manager receive input to the development of a Valuation Advisory improvement plan and the estimated completion dates/times of each activity?
<--- Score

38. What are the dynamics of the communication plan?
<--- Score

39. Is there a completed, verified, and validated high-level 'as is' (not 'should be' or 'could be') business process map?

<--- Score

40. Is the team adequately staffed with the desired cross-functionality? If not, what additional resources are available to the team?
<--- Score

41. What happens if Valuation Advisory's scope changes?
<--- Score

42. Has the Valuation Advisory work been fairly and/or equitably divided and delegated among team members who are qualified and capable to perform the work? Has everyone contributed?
<--- Score

43. Is the Valuation Advisory scope complete and appropriately sized?
<--- Score

44. How do you hand over Valuation Advisory context?
<--- Score

45. Is Valuation Advisory linked to key business goals and objectives?
<--- Score

46. When is the estimated completion date?
<--- Score

47. Is the improvement team aware of the different versions of a process: what they think it is vs. what it actually is vs. what it should be vs. what it could be?
<--- Score

48. How do you keep key subject matter experts in the loop?
<--- Score

49. Are team charters developed?
<--- Score

50. Is Valuation Advisory required?
<--- Score

51. What baselines are required to be defined and managed?
<--- Score

52. What would be the goal or target for a Valuation Advisory's improvement team?
<--- Score

53. Has the direction changed at all during the course of Valuation Advisory? If so, when did it change and why?
<--- Score

54. Has a high-level 'as is' process map been completed, verified and validated?
<--- Score

55. How can the value of Valuation Advisory be defined?
<--- Score

56. What defines best in class?
<--- Score

57. Are there any constraints known that bear on the

ability to perform Valuation Advisory work? How is the team addressing them?
<--- Score

58. How do you gather Valuation Advisory requirements?
<--- Score

59. Is full participation by members in regularly held team meetings guaranteed?
<--- Score

60. What are the rough order estimates on cost savings/opportunities that Valuation Advisory brings?
<--- Score

61. What is the definition of success?
<--- Score

62. How will the Valuation Advisory team and the organization measure complete success of Valuation Advisory?
<--- Score

63. Do you all define Valuation Advisory in the same way?
<--- Score

64. Is the Valuation Advisory scope manageable?
<--- Score

65. What is the context?
<--- Score

66. Are required metrics defined, what are they?
<--- Score

67. If substitutes have been appointed, have they been briefed on the Valuation Advisory goals and received regular communications as to the progress to date?
<--- Score

68. How will variation in the actual durations of each activity be dealt with to ensure that the expected Valuation Advisory results are met?
<--- Score

69. What is in the scope and what is not in scope?
<--- Score

70. What specifically is the problem? Where does it occur? When does it occur? What is its extent?
<--- Score

71. How was the 'as is' process map developed, reviewed, verified and validated?
<--- Score

72. Scope of sensitive information?
<--- Score

73. What critical content must be communicated – who, what, when, where, and how?
<--- Score

74. Have specific policy objectives been defined? .
<--- Score

75. Have all basic functions of Valuation Advisory been defined?
<--- Score

76. What are the record-keeping requirements of Valuation Advisory activities?
<--- Score

77. Has anyone else (internal or external to the organization) attempted to solve this problem or a similar one before? If so, what knowledge can be leveraged from these previous efforts?
<--- Score

78. Has a project plan, Gantt chart, or similar been developed/completed?
<--- Score

79. Are different versions of process maps needed to account for the different types of inputs?
<--- Score

80. What is the scope of Valuation Advisory?
<--- Score

81. Is the scope of Valuation Advisory defined?
<--- Score

82. Will team members perform Valuation Advisory work when assigned and in a timely fashion?
<--- Score

83. Has the improvement team collected the 'voice of the customer' (obtained feedback – qualitative and quantitative)?
<--- Score

84. Are business processes mapped?
<--- Score

85. Is data collected and displayed to better understand customer(s) critical needs and requirements.
<--- Score

86. How often are the team meetings?
<--- Score

87. How do you think the partners involved in Valuation Advisory would have defined success?
<--- Score

88. Have the customer needs been translated into specific, measurable requirements? How?
<--- Score

89. Is there a Valuation Advisory management charter, including business case, problem and goal statements, scope, milestones, roles and responsibilities, communication plan?
<--- Score

90. Is a fully trained team formed, supported, and committed to work on the Valuation Advisory improvements?
<--- Score

91. In what way can you redefine the criteria of choice clients have in your category in your favor?
<--- Score

92. Are there different segments of customers?
<--- Score

93. Has a team charter been developed and

communicated?

<--- Score

94. Is the team equipped with available and reliable resources?

<--- Score

95. Have all of the relationships been defined properly?

<--- Score

96. Is the team sponsored by a champion or business leader?

<--- Score

97. Does the team have regular meetings?

<--- Score

98. Are resources adequate for the scope?

<--- Score

99. Are accountability and ownership for Valuation Advisory clearly defined?

<--- Score

100. What key business process output measure(s) does Valuation Advisory leverage and how?

<--- Score

101. What are the compelling business reasons for embarking on Valuation Advisory?

<--- Score

102. Is there regularly 100% attendance at the team meetings? If not, have appointed substitutes attended to preserve cross-functionality and full

representation?

<--- Score

Add up total points for this section:

_ _ _ _ _ = Total points for this section

Divided by: _ _ _ _ _ _ (number of
statements answered) = _ _ _ _ _ _
Average score for this section

Transfer your score to the Valuation
Advisory Index at the beginning of the
Self-Assessment.

CRITERION #3: MEASURE:

In my belief, the answer to this
question is clearly defined:

5 Strongly Agree

4 Agree

3 Neutral

2 Disagree

1 Strongly Disagree

1. Are you taking your company in the direction of better and revenue or cheaper and cost?
<--- Score

2. What potential environmental factors impact the Valuation Advisory effort?
<--- Score

3. Does Valuation Advisory analysis show the

relationships among important Valuation Advisory factors?

<--- Score

4. How do you aggregate measures across priorities?

<--- Score

5. What do you measure and why?

<--- Score

6. Do staff have the necessary skills to collect, analyze, and report data?

<--- Score

7. Did you tackle the cause or the symptom?

<--- Score

8. Which measures and indicators matter?

<--- Score

9. Are the units of measure consistent?

<--- Score

10. Have changes been properly/adequately analyzed for effect?

<--- Score

11. What are the key input variables? What are the key process variables? What are the key output variables?

<--- Score

12. Have you found any 'ground fruit' or 'low-hanging fruit' for immediate remedies to the gap in performance?

<--- Score

13. What data was collected (past, present, future/ongoing)?
<--- Score

14. What are your customers expectations and measures?
<--- Score

15. What measurements are possible, practicable and meaningful?
<--- Score

16. How do you control the overall costs of your work processes?
<--- Score

17. How will success or failure be measured?
<--- Score

18. What are your key Valuation Advisory indicators that you will measure, analyze and track?
<--- Score

19. What relevant entities could be measured?
<--- Score

20. What disadvantage does this cause for the user?
<--- Score

21. How do you identify and analyze stakeholders and their interests?
<--- Score

22. Can you measure the return on analysis?
<--- Score

23. How do you measure lifecycle phases?
<--- Score

24. How will your organization measure success?
<--- Score

25. Is the solution cost-effective?
<--- Score

26. What is an unallowable cost?
<--- Score

27. Do you aggressively reward and promote the people who have the biggest impact on creating excellent Valuation Advisory services/products?
<--- Score

28. How do you measure efficient delivery of Valuation Advisory services?
<--- Score

29. Does Valuation Advisory systematically track and analyze outcomes for accountability and quality improvement?
<--- Score

30. What is the total cost related to deploying Valuation Advisory, including any consulting or professional services?
<--- Score

31. What evidence is there and what is measured?
<--- Score

32. Are missed Valuation Advisory opportunities costing your organization money?

<--- Score

33. How are measurements made?
<--- Score

34. Why do the measurements/indicators matter?
<--- Score

35. Are the measurements objective?
<--- Score

36. How do you do risk analysis of rare, cascading, catastrophic events?
<--- Score

37. How do you measure success?
<--- Score

38. Who participated in the data collection for measurements?
<--- Score

39. Among the Valuation Advisory product and service cost to be estimated, which is considered hardest to estimate?
<--- Score

40. What has the team done to assure the stability and accuracy of the measurement process?
<--- Score

41. How is the value delivered by Valuation Advisory being measured?
<--- Score

42. What could cause you to change course?

<--- Score

43. What charts has the team used to display the components of variation in the process?
<--- Score

44. How to cause the change?
<--- Score

45. Are process variation components displayed/communicated using suitable charts, graphs, plots?
<--- Score

46. What causes investor action?
<--- Score

47. How large is the gap between current performance and the customer-specified (goal) performance?
<--- Score

48. Where is it measured?
<--- Score

49. How will you measure success?
<--- Score

50. Have you made assumptions about the shape of the future, particularly its impact on your customers and competitors?
<--- Score

51. Is Process Variation Displayed/Communicated?
<--- Score

52. How is progress measured?

<--- Score

53. What causes innovation to fail or succeed in your organization?
<--- Score

54. What would be a real cause for concern?
<--- Score

55. Does your organization systematically track and analyze outcomes related for accountability and quality improvement?
<--- Score

56. What methods are feasible and acceptable to estimate the impact of reforms?
<--- Score

57. What are the types and number of measures to use?
<--- Score

58. What could cause delays in the schedule?
<--- Score

59. Is long term and short term variability accounted for?
<--- Score

60. Is it possible to estimate the impact of unanticipated complexity such as wrong or failed assumptions, feedback, etc. on proposed reforms?
<--- Score

61. What are the costs of reform?
<--- Score

62. Is data collection planned and executed?
<--- Score

63. Is a solid data collection plan established that includes measurement systems analysis?
<--- Score

64. What measurements are being captured?
<--- Score

65. What particular quality tools did the team find helpful in establishing measurements?
<--- Score

66. Does Valuation Advisory analysis isolate the fundamental causes of problems?
<--- Score

67. What causes extra work or rework?
<--- Score

68. Who should receive measurement reports?
<--- Score

69. How will measures be used to manage and adapt?
<--- Score

70. Are there any easy-to-implement alternatives to Valuation Advisory? Sometimes other solutions are available that do not require the cost implications of a full-blown project?
<--- Score

71. How is performance measured?
<--- Score

72. What causes mismanagement?
<--- Score

73. Is key measure data collection planned
and executed, process variation displayed and
communicated and performance baselined?
<--- Score

74. Will Valuation Advisory have an impact on current
business continuity, disaster recovery processes and/
or infrastructure?
<--- Score

75. What key measures identified indicate the
performance of the business process?
<--- Score

76. When is Root Cause Analysis Required?
<--- Score

77. Are key measures identified and agreed upon?
<--- Score

78. How will you measure your Valuation Advisory
effectiveness?
<--- Score

79. Can you do Valuation Advisory without complex
(expensive) analysis?
<--- Score

80. Is data collected on key measures that were
identified?
<--- Score

81. Are high impact defects defined and identified in the business process?
<--- Score

82. Is there a Performance Baseline?
<--- Score

83. Are losses documented, analyzed, and remedial processes developed to prevent future losses?
<--- Score

84. How do your measurements capture actionable Valuation Advisory information for use in exceeding your customers expectations and securing your customers engagement?
<--- Score

85. What is the right balance of time and resources between investigation, analysis, and discussion and dissemination?
<--- Score

86. Have the concerns of stakeholders to help identify and define potential barriers been obtained and analyzed?
<--- Score

87. Does the Valuation Advisory task fit the client's priorities?
<--- Score

88. What are the agreed upon definitions of the high impact areas, defect(s), unit(s), and opportunities that will figure into the process capability metrics?
<--- Score

89. What are your key Valuation Advisory organizational performance measures, including key short and longer-term financial measures?
<--- Score

90. Are you aware of what could cause a problem?
<--- Score

91. Was a data collection plan established?
<--- Score

92. How can you measure the performance?
<--- Score

Add up total points for this section:
_ _ _ _ _ = Total points for this section

Divided by: _ _ _ _ _ _ (number of statements answered) = _ _ _ _ _ _
Average score for this section

Transfer your score to the Valuation Advisory Index at the beginning of the Self-Assessment.

CRITERION #4: ANALYZE:

1. Was a cause-and-effect diagram used to explore the different types of causes (or sources of variation)?
<--- Score

2. Identify an operational issue in your organization. for example, could a particular task be done more quickly or more efficiently by Valuation Advisory?
<--- Score

3. Is the required Valuation Advisory data gathered?

<--- Score

4. When conducting a business process reengineering study, what do you look for when trying to identify business processes to change?
<--- Score

5. How do you identify specific Valuation Advisory investment opportunities and emerging trends?
<--- Score

6. What data is gathered?
<--- Score

7. How is the way you as the leader think and process information affecting your organizational culture?
<--- Score

8. What quality tools were used to get through the analyze phase?
<--- Score

9. What other organizational variables, such as reward systems or communication systems, affect the performance of this Valuation Advisory process?
<--- Score

10. Were any designed experiments used to generate additional insight into the data analysis?
<--- Score

11. A compounding model resolution with available relevant data can often provide insight towards a solution methodology; which Valuation Advisory models, tools and techniques are necessary?
<--- Score

12. What conclusions were drawn from the team's data collection and analysis? How did the team reach these conclusions?
<--- Score

13. How do you promote understanding that opportunity for improvement is not criticism of the status quo, or the people who created the status quo?
<--- Score

14. Do your leaders quickly bounce back from setbacks?
<--- Score

15. What tools were used to narrow the list of possible causes?
<--- Score

16. What are your current levels and trends in key Valuation Advisory measures or indicators of product and process performance that are important to and directly serve your customers?
<--- Score

17. What are the best opportunities for value improvement?
<--- Score

18. What are your key performance measures or indicators and in-process measures for the control and improvement of your Valuation Advisory processes?
<--- Score

19. Is Data and process analysis, root cause analysis

and quantifying the gap/opportunity in place?
<--- Score

20. Where is the data coming from to measure compliance?
<--- Score

21. Have any additional benefits been identified that will result from closing all or most of the gaps?
<--- Score

22. What process should you select for improvement?
<--- Score

23. What does the data say about the performance of the business process?
<--- Score

24. What tools were used to generate the list of possible causes?
<--- Score

25. What controls do you have in place to protect data?
<--- Score

26. How do you measure the operational performance of your key work systems and processes, including productivity, cycle time, and other appropriate measures of process effectiveness, efficiency, and innovation?
<--- Score

27. What are your current levels and trends in key measures or indicators of Valuation Advisory product and process performance that are important to and

directly serve your customers? How do these results compare with the performance of your competitors and other organizations with similar offerings?
<--- Score

28. What are your best practices for minimizing Valuation Advisory project risk, while demonstrating incremental value and quick wins throughout the Valuation Advisory project lifecycle?
<--- Score

29. How often will data be collected for measures?
<--- Score

30. Do you, as a leader, bounce back quickly from setbacks?
<--- Score

31. Were there any improvement opportunities identified from the process analysis?
<--- Score

32. How do mission and objectives affect the Valuation Advisory processes of your organization?
<--- Score

33. Did any value-added analysis or 'lean thinking' take place to identify some of the gaps shown on the 'as is' process map?
<--- Score

34. How do your work systems and key work processes relate to and capitalize on your core competencies?
<--- Score

35. Was a detailed process map created to amplify critical steps of the 'as is' business process?
<--- Score

36. Is the performance gap determined?
<--- Score

37. Did any additional data need to be collected?
<--- Score

38. How was the detailed process map generated, verified, and validated?
<--- Score

39. How does the organization define, manage, and improve its Valuation Advisory processes?
<--- Score

40. Is the suppliers process defined and controlled?
<--- Score

41. Do your contracts/agreements contain data security obligations?
<--- Score

42. How is Valuation Advisory data gathered?
<--- Score

43. What Valuation Advisory data do you gather or use now?
<--- Score

44. Are Valuation Advisory changes recognized early enough to be approved through the regular process?
<--- Score

45. Think about the functions involved in your Valuation Advisory project, what processes flow from these functions?
<--- Score

46. Have the problem and goal statements been updated to reflect the additional knowledge gained from the analyze phase?
<--- Score

47. What is the cost of poor quality as supported by the team's analysis?
<--- Score

48. Where is Valuation Advisory data gathered?
<--- Score

49. Were Pareto charts (or similar) used to portray the 'heavy hitters' (or key sources of variation)?
<--- Score

50. Do several people in different organizational units assist with the Valuation Advisory process?
<--- Score

51. How do you implement and manage your work processes to ensure that they meet design requirements?
<--- Score

52. Is the Valuation Advisory process severely broken such that a re-design is necessary?
<--- Score

53. What did the team gain from developing a sub-process map?

<--- Score

54. What is your organizations process which leads to recognition of value generation?
<--- Score

55. What were the financial benefits resulting from any 'ground fruit or low-hanging fruit' (quick fixes)?
<--- Score

56. Are gaps between current performance and the goal performance identified?
<--- Score

57. Can you add value to the current Valuation Advisory decision-making process (largely qualitative) by incorporating uncertainty modeling (more quantitative)?
<--- Score

58. Is the gap/opportunity displayed and communicated in financial terms?
<--- Score

59. What are the revised rough estimates of the financial savings/opportunity for Valuation Advisory improvements?
<--- Score

60. Do your employees have the opportunity to do what they do best everyday?
<--- Score

61. What were the crucial 'moments of truth' on the process map?
<--- Score

62. An organizationally feasible system request is one that considers the mission, goals and objectives of the organization. Key questions are: is the Valuation Advisory solution request practical and will it solve a problem or take advantage of an opportunity to achieve company goals?

<--- Score

63. What are your Valuation Advisory processes?

<--- Score

Add up total points for this section:

_ _ _ _ _ = Total points for this section

Divided by: _ _ _ _ _ _ (number of statements answered) = _ _ _ _ _ _

Average score for this section

Transfer your score to the Valuation Advisory Index at the beginning of the Self-Assessment.

CRITERION #5: IMPROVE:

INTENT: Develop a practical solution.
Innovate, establish and test the
solution and to measure the results.

In my belief, the answer to this
question is clearly defined:

5 Strongly Agree

4 Agree

3 Neutral

2 Disagree

1 Strongly Disagree

1. Is there a small-scale pilot for proposed improvement(s)? What conclusions were drawn from the outcomes of a pilot?
<--- Score

2. At what point will vulnerability assessments be performed once Valuation Advisory is put into production (e.g., ongoing Risk Management after implementation)?

<--- Score

3. Is there a cost/benefit analysis of optimal solution(s)?
<--- Score

4. Do you combine technical expertise with business knowledge and Valuation Advisory Key topics include lifecycles, development approaches, requirements and how to make a business case?
<--- Score

5. What can you do to improve?
<--- Score

6. Who will be responsible for documenting the Valuation Advisory requirements in detail?
<--- Score

7. How do you go about comparing Valuation Advisory approaches/solutions?
<--- Score

8. Are you assessing Valuation Advisory and risk?
<--- Score

9. How will the organization know that the solution worked?
<--- Score

10. How do you improve your likelihood of success ?
<--- Score

11. How did the team generate the list of possible solutions?
<--- Score

12. Does the goal represent a desired result that can be measured?
<--- Score

13. For decision problems, how do you develop a decision statement?
<--- Score

14. How do you define the solutions' scope?
<--- Score

15. Was a pilot designed for the proposed solution(s)?
<--- Score

16. What do you want to improve?
<--- Score

17. How will you know that you have improved?
<--- Score

18. Is the implementation plan designed?
<--- Score

19. Are improved process ('should be') maps modified based on pilot data and analysis?
<--- Score

20. Is the optimal solution selected based on testing and analysis?
<--- Score

21. Is the measure of success for Valuation Advisory understandable to a variety of people?
<--- Score

22. How can you improve performance?
<--- Score

23. How will the team or the process owner(s) monitor the implementation plan to see that it is working as intended?
<--- Score

24. Is a solution implementation plan established, including schedule/work breakdown structure, resources, risk management plan, cost/budget, and control plan?
<--- Score

25. How do you stay flexible and focused to recognize larger Valuation Advisory results?
<--- Score

26. How do you keep improving Valuation Advisory?
<--- Score

27. How do you decide how much to remunerate an employee?
<--- Score

28. Will the controls trigger any other risks?
<--- Score

29. How do the Valuation Advisory results compare with the performance of your competitors and other organizations with similar offerings?
<--- Score

30. What tools were used to evaluate the potential solutions?
<--- Score

31. Who controls key decisions that will be made?
<--- Score

32. Were any criteria developed to assist the team in testing and evaluating potential solutions?
<--- Score

33. What to do with the results or outcomes of measurements?
<--- Score

34. Are risk triggers captured?
<--- Score

35. What resources are required for the improvement efforts?
<--- Score

36. How risky is your organization?
<--- Score

37. What is the magnitude of the improvements?
<--- Score

38. How do you manage and improve your Valuation Advisory work systems to deliver customer value and achieve organizational success and sustainability?
<--- Score

39. What is the team's contingency plan for potential problems occurring in implementation?
<--- Score

40. Describe the design of the pilot and what tests were conducted, if any?

<--- Score

41. Are there any constraints (technical, political, cultural, or otherwise) that would inhibit certain solutions?
<--- Score

42. How will you know that a change is an improvement?
<--- Score

43. Is a contingency plan established?
<--- Score

44. How do you link measurement and risk?
<--- Score

45. How do you improve productivity?
<--- Score

46. Is the scope clearly documented?
<--- Score

47. What attendant changes will need to be made to ensure that the solution is successful?
<--- Score

48. How does the team improve its work?
<--- Score

49. How can skill-level changes improve Valuation Advisory?
<--- Score

50. Are new and improved process ('should be') maps developed?

<--- Score

51. How do you measure progress and evaluate training effectiveness?
<--- Score

52. What is the risk?
<--- Score

53. What communications are necessary to support the implementation of the solution?
<--- Score

54. How will you measure the results?
<--- Score

55. What were the underlying assumptions on the cost-benefit analysis?
<--- Score

56. What is the implementation plan?
<--- Score

57. What improvements have been achieved?
<--- Score

58. Is the solution technically practical?
<--- Score

59. Is supporting Valuation Advisory documentation required?
<--- Score

60. How do you improve Valuation Advisory service perception, and satisfaction?
<--- Score

61. Risk events: what are the things that could go wrong?
<--- Score

62. Who will be using the results of the measurement activities?
<--- Score

63. Do those selected for the Valuation Advisory team have a good general understanding of what Valuation Advisory is all about?
<--- Score

64. Risk Identification: What are the possible risk events your organization faces in relation to Valuation Advisory?
<--- Score

65. Is pilot data collected and analyzed?
<--- Score

66. Is there a high likelihood that any recommendations will achieve their intended results?
<--- Score

67. In the past few months, what is the smallest change you have made that has had the biggest positive result? What was it about that small change that produced the large return?
<--- Score

68. What needs improvement? Why?
<--- Score

69. How does the solution remove the key sources of

issues discovered in the analyze phase?
<--- Score

70. What tools were most useful during the improve phase?
<--- Score

71. What lessons, if any, from a pilot were incorporated into the design of the full-scale solution?
<--- Score

72. Are possible solutions generated and tested?
<--- Score

73. What tools were used to tap into the creativity and encourage 'outside the box' thinking?
<--- Score

74. How do you measure improved Valuation Advisory service perception, and satisfaction?
<--- Score

75. Can you identify any significant risks or exposures to Valuation Advisory third- parties (vendors, service providers, alliance partners etc) that concern you?
<--- Score

76. What actually has to improve and by how much?
<--- Score

77. What does the 'should be' process map/design look like?
<--- Score

78. What error proofing will be done to address some of the discrepancies observed in the 'as is' process?

<--- Score

79. Are the best solutions selected?
<--- Score

80. Can the solution be designed and implemented within an acceptable time period?
<--- Score

81. How will you know when its improved?
<--- Score

82. To what extent does management recognize Valuation Advisory as a tool to increase the results?
<--- Score

83. For estimation problems, how do you develop an estimation statement?
<--- Score

84. Explorations of the frontiers of Valuation Advisory will help you build influence, improve Valuation Advisory, optimize decision making, and sustain change, what is your approach?
<--- Score

85. What is Valuation Advisory's impact on utilizing the best solution(s)?
<--- Score

86. What went well, what should change, what can improve?
<--- Score

87. What are the implications of the one critical Valuation Advisory decision 10 minutes, 10 months,

and 10 years from now?
<--- Score

88. How do you measure risk?
<--- Score

89. Risk factors: what are the characteristics of Valuation Advisory that make it risky?
<--- Score

90. Who controls the risk?
<--- Score

91. Who are the people involved in developing and implementing Valuation Advisory?
<--- Score

92. What tools do you use once you have decided on a Valuation Advisory strategy and more importantly how do you choose?
<--- Score

93. Why improve in the first place?
<--- Score

Add up total points for this section:
_ _ _ _ _ = Total points for this section

Divided by: _ _ _ _ _ _ (number of statements answered) = _ _ _ _ _ _
Average score for this section

Transfer your score to the Valuation Advisory Index at the beginning of the Self-Assessment.

CRITERION #6: CONTROL:

INTENT: Implement the practical solution. Maintain the performance and correct possible complications.

In my belief, the answer to this question is clearly defined:

5 Strongly Agree

4 Agree

3 Neutral

2 Disagree

1 Strongly Disagree

1. Act/Adjust: What Do you Need to Do Differently?
<--- Score

2. Is there a recommended audit plan for routine surveillance inspections of Valuation Advisory's gains?
<--- Score

3. Are pertinent alerts monitored, analyzed and distributed to appropriate personnel?

<--- Score

4. Is there a Valuation Advisory Communication plan covering who needs to get what information when?
<--- Score

5. Are the planned controls in place?
<--- Score

6. Does a troubleshooting guide exist or is it needed?
<--- Score

7. How do senior leaders actions reflect a commitment to the organizations Valuation Advisory values?
<--- Score

8. Will the team be available to assist members in planning investigations?
<--- Score

9. What is the recommended frequency of auditing?
<--- Score

10. Who will be in control?
<--- Score

11. What are the known security controls?
<--- Score

12. Are operating procedures consistent?
<--- Score

13. Are new process steps, standards, and documentation ingrained into normal operations?
<--- Score

14. How is change control managed?
<--- Score

15. Are suggested corrective/restorative actions indicated on the response plan for known causes to problems that might surface?
<--- Score

16. Implementation Planning: is a pilot needed to test the changes before a full roll out occurs?
<--- Score

17. What other areas of the organization might benefit from the Valuation Advisory team's improvements, knowledge, and learning?
<--- Score

18. Are controls in place and consistently applied?
<--- Score

19. How will the process owner verify improvement in present and future sigma levels, process capabilities?
<--- Score

20. Who is the Valuation Advisory process owner?
<--- Score

21. Do the Valuation Advisory decisions you make today help people and the planet tomorrow?
<--- Score

22. What is the best design framework for Valuation Advisory organization now that, in a post industrial-age if the top-down, command and control model is no longer relevant?

<--- Score

23. How do you establish and deploy modified action plans if circumstances require a shift in plans and rapid execution of new plans?
<--- Score

24. Does Valuation Advisory appropriately measure and monitor risk?
<--- Score

25. What should you measure to verify efficiency gains?
<--- Score

26. Is a response plan established and deployed?
<--- Score

27. Does the response plan contain a definite closed loop continual improvement scheme (e.g., plan-do-check-act)?
<--- Score

28. What is your theory of human motivation, and how does your compensation plan fit with that view?
<--- Score

29. Is there a transfer of ownership and knowledge to process owner and process team tasked with the responsibilities.
<--- Score

30. How might the organization capture best practices and lessons learned so as to leverage improvements across the business?
<--- Score

31. What do your reports reflect?
<--- Score

32. Is there a documented and implemented monitoring plan?
<--- Score

33. Where do ideas that reach policy makers and planners as proposals for Valuation Advisory strengthening and reform actually originate?
<--- Score

34. How will new or emerging customer needs/requirements be checked/communicated to orient the process toward meeting the new specifications and continually reducing variation?
<--- Score

35. Is a response plan in place for when the input, process, or output measures indicate an 'out-of-control' condition?
<--- Score

36. Is new knowledge gained imbedded in the response plan?
<--- Score

37. Against what alternative is success being measured?
<--- Score

38. What key inputs and outputs are being measured on an ongoing basis?
<--- Score

39. Are there documented procedures?
<--- Score

40. How can you best use all of your knowledge repositories to enhance learning and sharing?
<--- Score

41. Can support from partners be adjusted?
<--- Score

42. Has the improved process and its steps been standardized?
<--- Score

43. How will input, process, and output variables be checked to detect for sub-optimal conditions?
<--- Score

44. Is there a standardized process?
<--- Score

45. How will the process owner and team be able to hold the gains?
<--- Score

46. Are you measuring, monitoring and predicting Valuation Advisory activities to optimize operations and profitability, and enhancing outcomes?
<--- Score

47. What can you control?
<--- Score

48. How do your controls stack up?
<--- Score

49. Have new or revised work instructions resulted?
<--- Score

50. Does the Valuation Advisory performance meet the customer's requirements?
<--- Score

51. How will the day-to-day responsibilities for monitoring and continual improvement be transferred from the improvement team to the process owner?
<--- Score

52. What other systems, operations, processes, and infrastructures (hiring practices, staffing, training, incentives/rewards, metrics/dashboards/scorecards, etc.) need updates, additions, changes, or deletions in order to facilitate knowledge transfer and improvements?
<--- Score

53. What are the critical parameters to watch?
<--- Score

54. What do you stand for--and what are you against?
<--- Score

55. Is knowledge gained on process shared and institutionalized?
<--- Score

56. Do you monitor the effectiveness of your Valuation Advisory activities?
<--- Score

57. How do you select, collect, align, and integrate

Valuation Advisory data and information for tracking daily operations and overall organizational performance, including progress relative to strategic objectives and action plans?
<--- Score

58. What are your results for key measures or indicators of the accomplishment of your Valuation Advisory strategy and action plans, including building and strengthening core competencies?
<--- Score

59. Is reporting being used or needed?
<--- Score

60. What do you measure to verify effectiveness gains?
<--- Score

61. What are the key elements of your Valuation Advisory performance improvement system, including your evaluation, organizational learning, and innovation processes?
<--- Score

62. What should the next improvement project be that is related to Valuation Advisory?
<--- Score

63. How do you plan on providing proper recognition and disclosure of supporting companies?
<--- Score

64. Is there documentation that will support the successful operation of the improvement?
<--- Score

65. Will existing staff require re-training, for example, to learn new business processes?
<--- Score

66. How do controls support value?
<--- Score

67. What quality tools were useful in the control phase?
<--- Score

68. Is there a control plan in place for sustaining improvements (short and long-term)?
<--- Score

69. Will any special training be provided for results interpretation?
<--- Score

70. What adjustments to the strategies are needed?
<--- Score

71. Does job training on the documented procedures need to be part of the process team's education and training?
<--- Score

72. Are the planned controls working?
<--- Score

73. How will you measure your QA plan's effectiveness?
<--- Score

74. Are documented procedures clear and easy to

follow for the operators?
<--- Score

75. How will report readings be checked to effectively monitor performance?
<--- Score

76. What are you attempting to measure/monitor?
<--- Score

77. Who controls critical resources?
<--- Score

78. What is the control/monitoring plan?
<--- Score

Add up total points for this section:
_ _ _ _ _   = Total points for this section

Divided by: _ _ _ _ _ _   (number of statements answered) = _ _ _ _ _ _
Average score for this section

Transfer your score to the Valuation Advisory Index at the beginning of the Self-Assessment.

CRITERION #7: SUSTAIN:

INTENT: Retain the benefits.

In my belief, the answer to this
question is clearly defined:

5 Strongly Agree

4 Agree

3 Neutral

2 Disagree

1 Strongly Disagree

1. How do you provide a safe environment -physically
and emotionally?
<--- Score

2. In the past year, what have you done (or could you
have done) to increase the accurate perception of
your company/brand as ethical and honest?
<--- Score

3. How do you create buy-in?
<--- Score

4. What must you excel at?
<--- Score

5. What business benefits will Valuation Advisory goals deliver if achieved?
<--- Score

6. Who will be responsible for deciding whether Valuation Advisory goes ahead or not after the initial investigations?
<--- Score

7. Which models, tools and techniques are necessary?
<--- Score

8. Is maximizing Valuation Advisory protection the same as minimizing Valuation Advisory loss?
<--- Score

9. Are you making progress, and are you making progress as Valuation Advisory leaders?
<--- Score

10. What are your most important goals for the strategic Valuation Advisory objectives?
<--- Score

11. How do you track customer value, profitability or financial return, organizational success, and sustainability?
<--- Score

12. Have benefits been optimized with all key stakeholders?
<--- Score

13. Who are four people whose careers you have enhanced?
<--- Score

14. Whom among your colleagues do you trust, and for what?
<--- Score

15. Do you have past Valuation Advisory successes?
<--- Score

16. What current systems have to be understood and/or changed?
<--- Score

17. What does your signature ensure?
<--- Score

18. How do senior leaders deploy your organizations vision and values through your leadership system, to the workforce, to key suppliers and partners, and to customers and other stakeholders, as appropriate?
<--- Score

19. Operational - will it work?
<--- Score

20. Are you paying enough attention to the partners your company depends on to succeed?
<--- Score

21. Has implementation been effective in reaching specified objectives so far?
<--- Score

22. What are the top 3 things at the forefront of your Valuation Advisory agendas for the next 3 years?
<--- Score

23. Can you break it down?
<--- Score

24. What are the long-term Valuation Advisory goals?
<--- Score

25. Why should you adopt a Valuation Advisory framework?
<--- Score

26. What have been your experiences in defining long range Valuation Advisory goals?
<--- Score

27. Which Valuation Advisory goals are the most important?
<--- Score

28. Is Valuation Advisory dependent on the successful delivery of a current project?
<--- Score

29. Is your strategy driving your strategy? Or is the way in which you allocate resources driving your strategy?
<--- Score

30. How do you make it meaningful in connecting Valuation Advisory with what users do day-to-day?
<--- Score

31. What are the rules and assumptions your industry

operates under? What if the opposite were true?
<--- Score

32. What would have to be true for the option on the table to be the best possible choice?
<--- Score

33. In retrospect, of the projects that you pulled the plug on, what percent do you wish had been allowed to keep going, and what percent do you wish had ended earlier?
<--- Score

34. What will drive Valuation Advisory change?
<--- Score

35. What Valuation Advisory skills are most important?
<--- Score

36. What happens if you do not have enough funding?
<--- Score

37. If you had to rebuild your organization without any traditional competitive advantages (i.e., no killer a technology, promising research, innovative product/ service delivery model, etc.), how would your people have to approach their work and collaborate together in order to create the necessary conditions for success?
<--- Score

38. Is your basic point _____ or _____?
<--- Score

39. Who is the main stakeholder, with ultimate

responsibility for driving Valuation Advisory forward?
<--- Score

40. Do you say no to customers for no reason?
<--- Score

41. How do you manage Valuation Advisory Knowledge Management (KM)?
<--- Score

42. Are you maintaining a past–present–future perspective throughout the Valuation Advisory discussion?
<--- Score

43. Will it be accepted by users?
<--- Score

44. How do you set Valuation Advisory stretch targets and how do you get people to not only participate in setting these stretch targets but also that they strive to achieve these?
<--- Score

45. Do Valuation Advisory rules make a reasonable demand on a users capabilities?
<--- Score

46. How likely is it that a customer would recommend your company to a friend or colleague?
<--- Score

47. When information truly is ubiquitous, when reach and connectivity are completely global, when computing resources are infinite, and when a whole new set of impossibilities are not only possible, but

happening, what will that do to your business?
<--- Score

48. Do you have the right capabilities and capacities?
<--- Score

49. What are the key enablers to make this Valuation Advisory move?
<--- Score

50. If you got fired and a new hire took your place, what would she do different?
<--- Score

51. What you are going to do to affect the numbers?
<--- Score

52. Are the assumptions believable and achievable?
<--- Score

53. If you weren't already in this business, would you enter it today? And if not, what are you going to do about it?
<--- Score

54. How do you lead with Valuation Advisory in mind?
<--- Score

55. Is it economical; do you have the time and money?
<--- Score

56. What information is critical to your organization that your executives are ignoring?
<--- Score

57. What is your question? Why?

<--- Score

58. Why should people listen to you?
<--- Score

59. Can you maintain your growth without detracting from the factors that have contributed to your success?
<--- Score

60. What Valuation Advisory modifications can you make work for you?
<--- Score

61. What unique value proposition (UVP) do you offer?
<--- Score

62. How will you ensure you get what you expected?
<--- Score

63. How do you foster innovation?
<--- Score

64. Can the schedule be done in the given time?
<--- Score

65. How does Valuation Advisory integrate with other business initiatives?
<--- Score

66. What is the overall business strategy?
<--- Score

67. What are the usability implications of Valuation Advisory actions?
<--- Score

68. Do you think you know, or do you know you know
?
<--- Score

69. How do you assess the Valuation Advisory pitfalls
that are inherent in implementing it?
<--- Score

70. What are the business goals Valuation Advisory is
aiming to achieve?
<--- Score

71. Are you / should you be revolutionary or
evolutionary?
<--- Score

72. How do you govern and fulfill your societal
responsibilities?
<--- Score

73. What projects are going on in the organization
today, and what resources are those projects using
from the resource pools?
<--- Score

74. Do you have an implicit bias for capital
investments over people investments?
<--- Score

75. Who is responsible for Valuation Advisory?
<--- Score

76. If there were zero limitations, what would you do
differently?
<--- Score

77. Did your employees make progress today?
<--- Score

78. How will you motivate the stakeholders with the least vested interest?
<--- Score

79. What kind of crime could a potential new hire have committed that would not only not disqualify him/her from being hired by your organization, but would actually indicate that he/she might be a particularly good fit?
<--- Score

80. Who will provide the final approval of Valuation Advisory deliverables?
<--- Score

81. What do we do when new problems arise?
<--- Score

82. What relationships among Valuation Advisory trends do you perceive?
<--- Score

83. What potential megatrends could make your business model obsolete?
<--- Score

84. To whom do you add value?
<--- Score

85. Are you satisfied with your current role? If not, what is missing from it?
<--- Score

86. Are all key stakeholders present at all Structured Walkthroughs?
<--- Score

87. What are internal and external Valuation Advisory relations?
<--- Score

88. What is the funding source for this project?
<--- Score

89. What trouble can you get into?
<--- Score

90. What is it like to work for you?
<--- Score

91. How important is Valuation Advisory to the user organizations mission?
<--- Score

92. How do you maintain Valuation Advisory's Integrity?
<--- Score

93. Is there any existing Valuation Advisory governance structure?
<--- Score

94. What is the source of the strategies for Valuation Advisory strengthening and reform?
<--- Score

95. What is the overall talent health of your organization as a whole at senior levels, and for each

organization reporting to a member of the Senior Leadership Team?
<--- Score

96. Who do you want your customers to become?
<--- Score

97. How do you listen to customers to obtain actionable information?
<--- Score

98. When you map the key players in your own work and the types/domains of relationships with them, which relationships do you find easy and which challenging, and why?
<--- Score

99. What management system can you use to leverage the Valuation Advisory experience, ideas, and concerns of the people closest to the work to be done?
<--- Score

100. Are you changing as fast as the world around you?
<--- Score

101. What is a feasible sequencing of reform initiatives over time?
<--- Score

102. Who have you, as a company, historically been when you've been at your best?
<--- Score

103. How is implementation research currently

incorporated into each of your goals?
<--- Score

104. How can you become more high-tech but still be high touch?
<--- Score

105. What was the last experiment you ran?
<--- Score

106. How do you proactively clarify deliverables and Valuation Advisory quality expectations?
<--- Score

107. Why is Valuation Advisory important for you now?
<--- Score

108. Who are the key stakeholders?
<--- Score

109. How do you transition from the baseline to the target?
<--- Score

110. If you had to leave your organization for a year and the only communication you could have with employees/colleagues was a single paragraph, what would you write?
<--- Score

111. How much contingency will be available in the budget?
<--- Score

112. What should you stop doing?

<--- Score

113. What are you challenging?
<--- Score

114. How can you negotiate Valuation Advisory successfully with a stubborn boss, an irate client, or a deceitful coworker?
<--- Score

115. How can you incorporate support to ensure safe and effective use of Valuation Advisory into the services that you provide?
<--- Score

116. Are new benefits received and understood?
<--- Score

117. What are current Valuation Advisory paradigms?
<--- Score

118. Do you have enough freaky customers in your portfolio pushing you to the limit day in and day out?
<--- Score

119. What are strategies for increasing support and reducing opposition?
<--- Score

120. What is your BATNA (best alternative to a negotiated agreement)?
<--- Score

121. What is the estimated value of the project?
<--- Score

122. How do you stay inspired?
<--- Score

123. What are your personal philosophies regarding Valuation Advisory and how do they influence your work?
<--- Score

124. What threat is Valuation Advisory addressing?
<--- Score

125. Which functions and people interact with the supplier and or customer?
<--- Score

126. Why not do Valuation Advisory?
<--- Score

127. Is the impact that Valuation Advisory has shown?
<--- Score

128. What is the purpose of Valuation Advisory in relation to the mission?
<--- Score

129. What are the gaps in your knowledge and experience?
<--- Score

130. How do you accomplish your long range Valuation Advisory goals?
<--- Score

131. Political -is anyone trying to undermine this project?
<--- Score

132. Ask yourself: how would you do this work if you only had one staff member to do it?
<--- Score

133. What will be the consequences to the stakeholder (financial, reputation etc) if Valuation Advisory does not go ahead or fails to deliver the objectives?
<--- Score

134. How much does Valuation Advisory help?
<--- Score

135. If your company went out of business tomorrow, would anyone who doesn't get a paycheck here care?
<--- Score

136. Who uses your product in ways you never expected?
<--- Score

137. Is there any reason to believe the opposite of my current belief?
<--- Score

138. What is the craziest thing you can do?
<--- Score

139. What is effective Valuation Advisory?
<--- Score

140. Why is it important to have senior management support for a Valuation Advisory project?
<--- Score

141. Were lessons learned captured and communicated?
<--- Score

142. What are the success criteria that will indicate that Valuation Advisory objectives have been met and the benefits delivered?
<--- Score

143. Do you see more potential in people than they do in themselves?
<--- Score

144. What trophy do you want on your mantle?
<--- Score

145. Is the Valuation Advisory organization completing tasks effectively and efficiently?
<--- Score

146. What goals did you miss?
<--- Score

147. What is your formula for success in Valuation Advisory ?
<--- Score

148. Who are your customers?
<--- Score

149. What is your competitive advantage?
<--- Score

150. How do you cross-sell and up-sell your Valuation Advisory success?
<--- Score

151. Why do and why don't your customers like your organization?
<--- Score

152. Think of your Valuation Advisory project, what are the main functions?
<--- Score

153. What may be the consequences for the performance of an organization if all stakeholders are not consulted regarding Valuation Advisory?
<--- Score

154. What are specific Valuation Advisory rules to follow?
<--- Score

155. If no one would ever find out about your accomplishments, how would you lead differently?
<--- Score

156. Who is responsible for ensuring appropriate resources (time, people and money) are allocated to Valuation Advisory?
<--- Score

157. How do you know if you are successful?
<--- Score

158. Who will determine interim and final deadlines?
<--- Score

159. What would you recommend your friend do if he/she were facing this dilemma?
<--- Score

160. How do you foster the skills, knowledge, talents, attributes, and characteristics you want to have?
<--- Score

161. How are you doing compared to your industry?
<--- Score

162. How do you engage the workforce, in addition to satisfying them?
<--- Score

163. What are the essentials of internal Valuation Advisory management?
<--- Score

164. What are the potential basics of Valuation Advisory fraud?
<--- Score

165. What are you trying to prove to yourself, and how might it be hijacking your life and business success?
<--- Score

166. Who do we want your customers to become?
<--- Score

167. Are assumptions made in Valuation Advisory stated explicitly?
<--- Score

168. Who do you think the world wants your organization to be?
<--- Score

169. What is the recommended frequency of auditing?

<--- Score

170. Do you know what you are doing? And who do you call if you don't?
<--- Score

171. Among your stronger employees, how many see themselves at the company in three years? How many would leave for a 10 percent raise from another company?
<--- Score

172. If your customer were your grandmother, would you tell her to buy what you're selling?
<--- Score

173. Is a Valuation Advisory team work effort in place?
<--- Score

174. Who, on the executive team or the board, has spoken to a customer recently?
<--- Score

175. Do you feel that more should be done in the Valuation Advisory area?
<--- Score

176. Instead of going to current contacts for new ideas, what if you reconnected with dormant contacts--the people you used to know? If you were going reactivate a dormant tie, who would it be?
<--- Score

177. At what moment would you think; Will I get fired?
<--- Score

178. Are you relevant? Will you be relevant five years from now? Ten?
<--- Score

179. What is the kind of project structure that would be appropriate for your Valuation Advisory project, should it be formal and complex, or can it be less formal and relatively simple?
<--- Score

180. What new services of functionality will be implemented next with Valuation Advisory ?
<--- Score

181. Which individuals, teams or departments will be involved in Valuation Advisory?
<--- Score

182. What knowledge, skills and characteristics mark a good Valuation Advisory project manager?
<--- Score

183. What are the barriers to increased Valuation Advisory production?
<--- Score

184. Do you know who is a friend or a foe?
<--- Score

185. Who else should you help?
<--- Score

186. How do you keep records, of what?
<--- Score

187. Who is responsible for errors?

<--- Score

188. What are the short and long-term Valuation Advisory goals?
<--- Score

189. How do you keep the momentum going?
<--- Score

190. Are there any disadvantages to implementing Valuation Advisory? There might be some that are less obvious?
<--- Score

191. Have new benefits been realized?
<--- Score

192. If you were responsible for initiating and implementing major changes in your organization, what steps might you take to ensure acceptance of those changes?
<--- Score

193. Can you do all this work?
<--- Score

Add up total points for this section:
_ _ _ _ _ = Total points for this section

Divided by: _ _ _ _ _ _ (number of statements answered) = _ _ _ _ _ _
Average score for this section

Transfer your score to the Valuation Advisory Index at the beginning of the Self-Assessment.

Valuation Advisory and Managing Projects, Criteria for Project Managers:

1.0 Initiating Process Group: Valuation Advisory

1. Have requirements been tested, approved, and fulfill the Valuation Advisory project scope?

2. Were resources available as planned?

3. What must be done?

4. What were the challenges that you encountered during the execution of a previous Valuation Advisory project that you would not want to repeat?

5. How do you help others satisfy needs?

6. Are identified risks being monitored properly, are new risks arising during the Valuation Advisory project or are foreseen risks occurring?

7. What are the inputs required to produce the deliverables?

8. Are the changes in your Valuation Advisory project being formally requested, analyzed, and approved by the appropriate decision makers?

9. Who is performing the work of the Valuation Advisory project?

10. Do you understand the communication expectations for this Valuation Advisory project?

11. What do they need to know about the Valuation Advisory project?

12. Were escalated issues resolved promptly?

13. Professionals want to know what is expected from them what are the deliverables?

14. What is the NEXT thing to do?

15. For technology Valuation Advisory projects only: Are all production support stakeholders (Business unit, technical support, & user) prepared for implementation with appropriate contingency plans?

16. At which cmmi level are software processes documented, standardized, and integrated into a standard to-be practiced process for your organization?

17. Just how important is your work to the overall success of the Valuation Advisory project?

18. What are the constraints?

19. What are the short and long term implications?

20. How well did the chosen processes produce the expected results?

1.1 Project Charter: Valuation Advisory

21. Why have you chosen the aim you have set forth?

22. When do you use a Valuation Advisory project Charter?

23. Does the Valuation Advisory project need to consider any special capacity or capability issues?

24. What barriers do you predict to your success?

25. What date will the task finish?

26. What are the known stakeholder requirements?

27. Fit with other Products Compliments – Cannibalizes?

28. Will this replace an existing product?

29. What are the deliverables?

30. For whom?

31. What is the business need?

32. What are the assigned resources?

33. Where does all this information come from?

34. Who will take notes, document decisions?

35. Is time of the essence?

36. How high should you set your goals?

37. What metrics could you look at?

38. Run it as as a startup?

39. Customer benefits: what customer requirements does this Valuation Advisory project address?

40. Must Have?

1.2 Stakeholder Register: Valuation Advisory

41. How will reports be created?

42. What & Why?

43. Who are the stakeholders?

44. What opportunities exist to provide communications?

45. How big is the gap?

46. What are the major Valuation Advisory project milestones requiring communications or providing communications opportunities?

47. Who is managing stakeholder engagement?

48. How should employers make voices heard?

49. What is the power of the stakeholder?

50. Who wants to talk about Security?

51. Is your organization ready for change?

52. How much influence do they have on the Valuation Advisory project?

1.3 Stakeholder Analysis Matrix: Valuation Advisory

53. Who is most interested in information about the topic and/or has previously initiated interest?

54. Are there people who ise voices or interests in the issue may not be heard?

55. New technologies, services, ideas?

56. Who will obstruct/hinder the Valuation Advisory project if they are not involved?

57. Price, value, quality?

58. How to measure the achievement of the Immediate Objective?

59. Gaps in capabilities?

60. What makes a person a stakeholder?

61. What advantages do your organizations stakeholders have?

62. Will the impacts be local, national or international?

63. How do rules, behaviors affect stakes?

64. What are the mechanisms of public and social accountability, and how can they be made better?

65. Reliability of data, plan predictability?

66. Where are the good opportunities facing your organizations development?

67. Contributions to policy and practice?

68. Legislative effects?

69. Disadvantages of proposition?

70. Competitors vulnerabilities?

71. How are you predicting what future (work)loads will be?

72. What is your organizations competitors doing?

2.0 Planning Process Group: Valuation Advisory

73. Who are the Valuation Advisory project stakeholders?

74. If task x starts two days late, what is the effect on the Valuation Advisory project end date?

75. What is involved in Valuation Advisory project scope management, and why is good Valuation Advisory project scope management so important on information technology Valuation Advisory projects?

76. If a task is partitionable, is this a sufficient condition to reduce the Valuation Advisory project duration?

77. Does the program have follow-up mechanisms (to verify the quality of the products, punctuality of delivery, etc.) to measure progress in the achievement of the envisaged results?

78. How can you make your needs known?

79. What is the difference between the early schedule and late schedule?

80. How are it Valuation Advisory projects different?

81. The Valuation Advisory project charter is created in which Valuation Advisory project management process group?

82. In which Valuation Advisory project management process group is the detailed Valuation Advisory project budget created?

83. Mitigate. what will you do to minimize the impact should a risk event occur?

84. Why do it Valuation Advisory projects fail?

85. In what way has the program contributed towards the issue culture and development included on the public agenda?

86. How well defined and documented are the Valuation Advisory project management processes you chose to use?

87. To what extent are the visions and actions of the partners consistent or divergent with regard to the program?

88. What input will you be required to provide the Valuation Advisory project team?

89. What should you do next?

90. To what extent has a PMO contributed to raising the quality of the design of the Valuation Advisory project?

91. What type of estimation method are you using?

92. Will the products created live up to the necessary quality?

2.1 Project Management Plan: Valuation Advisory

93. What is Valuation Advisory project scope management?

94. Are there non-structural buyout or relocation recommendations?

95. What did not work so well?

96. If the Valuation Advisory project management plan is a comprehensive document that guides you in Valuation Advisory project execution and control, then what should it NOT contain?

97. What data/reports/tools/etc. do your PMs need?

98. Who is the Valuation Advisory project Manager?

99. What happened during the process that you found interesting?

100. Are the proposed Valuation Advisory project purposes different than a previously authorized Valuation Advisory project?

101. Are the existing and future without-plan conditions reasonable and appropriate?

102. Are there any client staffing expectations?

103. Are comparable cost estimates used for

comparing, screening and selecting alternative plans, and has a reasonable cost estimate been developed for the recommended plan?

104. Was the peer (technical) review of the cost estimates duly coordinated with the cost estimate center of expertise and addressed in the review documentation and certification?

105. Is the appropriate plan selected based on your organizations objectives and evaluation criteria expressed in Principles and Guidelines policies?

106. Is mitigation authorized or recommended?

107. Does the implementation plan have an appropriate division of responsibilities?

108. What would you do differently what did not work?

109. Who is the sponsor?

110. Will you add a schedule and diagram?

2.2 Scope Management Plan: Valuation Advisory

111. Is each item clearly and completely defined?

112. For which criterion is it tolerable not to meet the original parameters?

113. Are stakeholders aware and supportive of the principles and practices of modern software estimation?

114. What threats might prevent you from getting there?

115. Function of the configuration control board?

116. Are trade-offs between accepting the risk and mitigating the risk identified?

117. Is your organization structure for both tracking & controlling the budget well defined and assigned to a specific individual?

118. Are vendor contract reports, reviews and visits conducted periodically?

119. What are the Quality Assurance overheads?

120. Have all involved Valuation Advisory project stakeholders and work groups committed to the Valuation Advisory project?

121. Have key stakeholders been identified?

122. How do you know how you are doing?

123. Do you document disagreements and work towards resolutions?

124. Has a quality assurance plan been developed for the Valuation Advisory project?

125. Describe the process for rejecting the Valuation Advisory project deliverables. What happens to rejected deliverables?

126. Has a resource management plan been created?

127. Is there a Valuation Advisory project organization chart showing the reporting relationships and responsibilities for each position?

128. Will the Valuation Advisory project deliverables become accepted in writing?

129. Have Valuation Advisory project team accountabilities & responsibilities been clearly defined?

130. Are staffing resource estimates sufficiently detailed and documented for use in planning and tracking the Valuation Advisory project?

2.3 Requirements Management Plan: Valuation Advisory

131. How knowledgeable is the primary Stakeholder(s) in the proposed application area?

132. Who is responsible for quantifying the Valuation Advisory project requirements?

133. If it exists, where is it housed?

134. Is any organizational data being used or stored?

135. Do you have price sheets and a methodology for determining the total proposal cost?

136. How will you develop the schedule of requirements activities?

137. What is the earliest finish date for this Valuation Advisory project if it is scheduled to start on ...?

138. Why manage requirements?

139. To see if a requirement statement is sufficiently well-defined, read it from the developers perspective. Mentally add the phrase, call me when youre done to the end of the requirement and see if that makes you nervous. In other words, would you need additional clarification from the author to understand the requirement well enough to design and implement it?

140. Who will approve the requirements (and if

multiple approvers, in what order)?

141. Will you use an assessment of the Valuation Advisory project environment as a tool to discover risk to the requirements process?

142. What went right?

143. Business analysis scope?

144. Who will initially review the Valuation Advisory project work or products to ensure it meets the applicable acceptance criteria?

145. Who is responsible for monitoring and tracking the Valuation Advisory project requirements?

146. Did you avoid subjective, flowery or non-specific statements?

147. Subject to change control?

148. Will the contractors involved take full responsibility?

149. How detailed should the Valuation Advisory project get?

150. Who has the authority to reject Valuation Advisory project requirements?

2.4 Requirements Documentation: Valuation Advisory

151. What are the attributes of a customer?

152. What can tools do for us?

153. What images does it conjure?

154. What is effective documentation?

155. How do you know when a Requirement is accurate enough?

156. Do technical resources exist?

157. What are the potential disadvantages/ advantages?

158. What will be the integration problems?

159. Are there legal issues?

160. What are the acceptance criteria?

161. How will the proposed Valuation Advisory project help?

162. Where do you define what is a customer, what are the attributes of customer?

163. If applicable; are there issues linked with the fact that this is an offshore Valuation Advisory project?

164. Is new technology needed?

165. Does your organization restrict technical alternatives?

166. Does the system provide the functions which best support the customers needs?

167. Who provides requirements?

168. Where are business rules being captured?

169. How much testing do you need to do to prove that your system is safe?

170. Is your business case still valid?

2.5 Requirements Traceability Matrix: Valuation Advisory

171. Will you use a Requirements Traceability Matrix?

172. How will it affect the stakeholders personally in their career?

173. What is the WBS?

174. Do you have a clear understanding of all subcontracts in place?

175. Is there a requirements traceability process in place?

176. Why use a WBS?

177. What percentage of Valuation Advisory projects are producing traceability matrices between requirements and other work products?

178. Describe the process for approving requirements so they can be added to the traceability matrix and Valuation Advisory project work can be performed. Will the Valuation Advisory project requirements become approved in writing?

179. Why do you manage scope?

180. What are the chronologies, contingencies, consequences, criteria?

181. How do you manage scope?

182. How small is small enough?

2.6 Project Scope Statement: Valuation Advisory

183. How will you haverify the accuracy of the work of the Valuation Advisory project, and what constitutes acceptance of the deliverables?

184. Will the risk status be reported to management on a regular and frequent basis?

185. Were potential customers involved early in the planning process?

186. Once its defined, what is the stability of the Valuation Advisory project scope?

187. Will an issue form be in use?

188. Risks?

189. Is the Valuation Advisory project organization documented and on file?

190. Does the scope statement still need some clarity?

191. Is the scope of your Valuation Advisory project well defined?

192. Has the Valuation Advisory project scope statement been reviewed as part of the baseline process?

193. Has everyone approved the Valuation Advisory

projects scope statement?

194. What is the most common tool for helping define the detail?

195. Is an issue management process documented and filed?

196. Elements that deal with providing the detail?

197. Is the change control process documented and on file?

198. Are the input requirements from the team members clearly documented and communicated?

199. Will statistics related to QA be collected, trends analyzed, and problems raised as issues?

200. Are the meetings set up to have assigned note takers that will add action/issues to the issue list?

201. How often will scope changes be reviewed?

2.7 Assumption and Constraint Log: Valuation Advisory

202. What is positive about the current process?

203. Can you perform this task or activity in a more effective manner?

204. Are processes for release management of new development from coding and unit testing, to integration testing, to training, and production defined and followed?

205. Does the plan conform to standards?

206. Is the steering committee active in Valuation Advisory project oversight?

207. Is the amount of effort justified by the anticipated value of forming a new process?

208. What worked well?

209. Have all involved stakeholders and work groups committed to the Valuation Advisory project?

210. Are you meeting your customers expectations consistently?

211. Contradictory information between different documents?

212. Does a documented Valuation Advisory project

organizational policy & plan (i.e. governance model) exist?

213. Has a Valuation Advisory project Communications Plan been developed?

214. Do you know what your customers expectations are regarding this process?

215. Are there cosmetic errors that hinder readability and comprehension?

216. Are there processes defining how software will be developed including development methods, overall timeline for development, software product standards, and traceability?

217. What to do at recovery?

218. After observing execution of process, is it in compliance with the documented Plan?

219. What do you audit?

220. Do the requirements meet the standards of correctness, completeness, consistency, accuracy, and readability?

221. How can you prevent/fix violations?

2.8 Work Breakdown Structure: Valuation Advisory

222. Is the work breakdown structure (wbs) defined and is the scope of the Valuation Advisory project clear with assigned deliverable owners?

223. How will you and your Valuation Advisory project team define the Valuation Advisory projects scope and work breakdown structure?

224. Why would you develop a Work Breakdown Structure?

225. How big is a work-package?

226. Where does it take place?

227. Why is it useful?

228. When do you stop?

229. How far down?

230. What is the probability that the Valuation Advisory project duration will exceed xx weeks?

231. Is it still viable?

232. When would you develop a Work Breakdown Structure?

233. Who has to do it?

234. What is the probability of completing the Valuation Advisory project in less that xx days?

235. How many levels?

236. Is it a change in scope?

237. Can you make it?

238. Do you need another level?

239. When does it have to be done?

240. What has to be done?

241. How much detail?

2.9 WBS Dictionary: Valuation Advisory

242. Does the contractor have procedures which permit identification of recurring or non-recurring costs as necessary?

243. What are you counting on?

244. Is work progressively subdivided into detailed work packages as requirements are defined?

245. Are the requirements for all items of overhead established by rational, traceable processes?

246. Does the scheduling system identify in a timely manner the status of work?

247. Are retroactive changes to budgets for completed work specifically prohibited in an established procedure, and is this procedure adhered to?

248. Identify potential or actual budget-based and time-based schedule variances?

249. Are work packages reasonably short in time duration or do they have adequate objective indicators/milestones to minimize subjectivity of the in process work evaluation?

250. Are meaningful indicators identified for use in measuring the status of cost and schedule

performance?

251. Identify and isolate causes of favorable and unfavorable cost and schedule variances?

252. Can the contractor substantiate work package and planning package budgets?

253. Budgets assigned to control accounts?

254. Is authorization of budgets in excess of the contract budget base controlled formally and done with the full knowledge and recognition of the procuring activity?

255. Are management actions taken to reduce indirect costs when there are significant adverse variances?

256. Are data elements (BCWS, BCWP, and ACWP) progressively summarized from the detail level to the contract level through the CWBS?

257. Are the variances between budgeted and actual indirect costs identified and analyzed at the level of assigned responsibility for control (indirect pool, department, etc.)?

258. Major functional areas of contract effort?

259. Is cost and schedule performance measurement done in a consistent, systematic manner?

2.10 Schedule Management Plan: Valuation Advisory

260. Is there an issues management plan in place?

261. Are meeting minutes captured and sent out after the meeting?

262. Is a payment system in place with proper reviews and approvals?

263. Is a process defined for baseline approval and control?

264. Will rolling way planning be used?

265. Are the activity durations realistic and at an appropriate level of detail for effective management?

266. Does all Valuation Advisory project documentation reside in a common repository for easy access?

267. Is quality monitored from the perspective of the customers needs and expectations?

268. Is there a requirements change management processes in place?

269. Are meeting objectives identified for each meeting?

270. Will the Valuation Advisory project sponsor be

involved in preliminary schedule reviews?

271. Goal: is the schedule feasible and at what cost?

272. Has your organization readiness assessment been conducted?

273. Pareto diagrams, statistical sampling, flow charting or trend analysis used quality monitoring?

274. Has a Valuation Advisory project Communications Plan been developed?

275. Have Valuation Advisory project team accountabilities & responsibilities been clearly defined?

276. Define units of measurement for each resource. For example, are you referencing gallons or liters?

277. Is there a formal process for updating the Valuation Advisory project baseline?

278. Is the assigned Valuation Advisory project manager a PMP (Certified Valuation Advisory project manager) and experienced?

279. Is stakeholder involvement adequate?

2.11 Activity List: Valuation Advisory

280. How do you determine the late start (LS) for each activity?

281. When will the work be performed?

282. What is the total time required to complete the Valuation Advisory project if no delays occur?

283. Should you include sub-activities?

284. What are the critical bottleneck activities?

285. What did not go as well?

286. Is infrastructure setup part of your Valuation Advisory project?

287. The wbs is developed as part of a joint planning session. and how do you know that youhave done this right?

288. What is the LF and LS for each activity?

289. What went wrong?

290. How much slack is available in the Valuation Advisory project?

291. What will be performed?

292. Can you determine the activity that must finish, before this activity can start?

293. How can the Valuation Advisory project be displayed graphically to better visualize the activities?

294. In what sequence?

295. For other activities, how much delay can be tolerated?

296. Who will perform the work?

297. How detailed should a Valuation Advisory project get?

2.12 Activity Attributes: Valuation Advisory

298. Why?

299. Which method produces the more accurate cost assignment?

300. Is there a trend during the year?

301. Can more resources be added?

302. Activity: what is In the Bag?

303. Have constraints been applied to the start and finish milestones for the phases?

304. Resource is assigned to?

305. Can you re-assign any activities to another resource to resolve an over-allocation?

306. How difficult will it be to do specific activities on this Valuation Advisory project?

307. Time for overtime?

308. Activity: fair or not fair?

309. Would you consider either of corresponding activities an outlier?

310. Is there anything planned that does not need to

be here?

311. Are the required resources available or need to be acquired?

312. What is your organizations history in doing similar activities?

313. Do you feel very comfortable with your prediction?

314. Have you identified the Activity Leveling Priority code value on each activity?

315. How many resources do you need to complete the work scope within a limit of X number of days?

316. Where else does it apply?

2.13 Milestone List: Valuation Advisory

317. Sustainable financial backing?

318. Can you derive how soon can the whole Valuation Advisory project finish?

319. Obstacles faced?

320. Timescales, deadlines and pressures?

321. Information and research?

322. What is the market for your technology, product or service?

323. Milestone pages should display the UserID of the person who added the milestone. Does a report or query exist that provides this audit information?

324. Do you foresee any technical risks or developmental challenges?

325. Own known vulnerabilities?

326. What background experience, skills, and strengths does the team bring to your organization?

327. Continuity, supply chain robustness?

328. Competitive advantages?

329. Global influences?

330. Usps (unique selling points)?

331. Effects on core activities, distraction?

332. Sustaining internal capabilities?

333. How difficult will it be to do specific activities on this Valuation Advisory project?

2.14 Network Diagram: Valuation Advisory

334. How difficult will it be to do specific activities on this Valuation Advisory project?

335. What can be done concurrently?

336. Where do you schedule uncertainty time?

337. What are the tools?

338. What to do and When?

339. What is the lowest cost to complete this Valuation Advisory project in xx weeks?

340. What are the Major Administrative Issues?

341. What controls the start and finish of a job?

342. Can you calculate the confidence level?

343. What job or jobs could run concurrently?

344. What job or jobs follow it?

345. How confident can you be in your milestone dates and the delivery date?

346. Where do schedules come from?

347. Planning: who, how long, what to do?

348. What activity must be completed immediately before this activity can start?

349. Exercise: what is the probability that the Valuation Advisory project duration will exceed xx weeks?

350. Review the logical flow of the network diagram. Take a look at which activities you have first and then sequence the activities. Do they make sense?

351. What activities must occur simultaneously with this activity?

352. Which type of network diagram allows you to depict four types of dependencies?

2.15 Activity Resource Requirements: Valuation Advisory

353. Do you use tools like decomposition and rolling-wave planning to produce the activity list and other outputs?

354. Which logical relationship does the PDM use most often?

355. Other support in specific areas?

356. How do you manage time?

357. What are constraints that you might find during the Human Resource Planning process?

358. Anything else?

359. Are there unresolved issues that need to be addressed?

360. How many signatures do you require on a check and does this match what is in your policy and procedures?

361. How do you handle petty cash?

362. When does monitoring begin?

363. What is the Work Plan Standard?

364. Organizational Applicability?

365. Why do you do that?

2.16 Resource Breakdown Structure: Valuation Advisory

366. Who will use the system?

367. Who is allowed to see what data about which resources?

368. Any changes from stakeholders?

369. Are the required resources available?

370. What can you do to improve productivity?

371. Why time management?

372. What is the difference between % Complete and % work?

373. Why is this important?

374. What is the primary purpose of the human resource plan?

375. What is the purpose of assigning and documenting responsibility?

376. What defines a successful Valuation Advisory project?

377. Who needs what information?

378. Who is allowed to perform which functions?

379. When do they need the information?

380. How should the information be delivered?

381. Who will be used as a Valuation Advisory project team member?

2.17 Activity Duration Estimates: Valuation Advisory

382. Do procedures exist that identify when and how human resources are introduced and removed from the Valuation Advisory project?

383. What are the main types of contracts if you do decide to outsource?

384. Is the work performed reviewed against contractual objectives?

385. How many different communications channels does a Valuation Advisory project team with six people have?

386. How do theories relate to Valuation Advisory project management?

387. Do you think Valuation Advisory project managers of large information technology Valuation Advisory projects need strong technical skills?

388. Does the software appear easy to learn?

389. How does Valuation Advisory project integration management relate to the Valuation Advisory project life cycle, stakeholders, and the other Valuation Advisory project management knowledge areas?

390. What tasks can take place concurrently?

391. When a risk event occurs, is the risk response evaluated and the appropriate response implemented?

392. Do Valuation Advisory project team members work in the same physical location to enhance team performance?

393. What is done after activity duration estimation?

394. Are inspections completed to determine if the results comply with the requirements?

395. Is a standard form used to obtain bids and proposals from prospective sellers?

396. How have experts such as Deming, Juran, Crosby, and Taguchi affected the quality movement and todays use of Six Sigma?

397. Are activity dependencies identified?

398. Briefly summarize the work done by Maslow, Herzberg, McClellan, McGregor, Ouchi, Thamhain and Wilemon, and Covey. How do theories relate to Valuation Advisory project management?

399. Research recruiting and retention strategies at three different companies. What distinguishes one organization from another in this area?

400. Do you agree with the suggestions provided for improving Valuation Advisory project communications?

401. What is the duration of a milestone?

2.18 Duration Estimating Worksheet: Valuation Advisory

402. When, then?

403. What info is needed?

404. Will the Valuation Advisory project collaborate with the local community and leverage resources?

405. Can the Valuation Advisory project be constructed as planned?

406. How can the Valuation Advisory project be displayed graphically to better visualize the activities?

407. What is your role?

408. How should ongoing costs be monitored to try to keep the Valuation Advisory project within budget?

409. What is cost and Valuation Advisory project cost management?

410. Why estimate costs?

411. Does the Valuation Advisory project provide innovative ways for stakeholders to overcome obstacles or deliver better outcomes?

412. What is next?

413. What utility impacts are there?

414. What work will be included in the Valuation Advisory project?

415. What questions do you have?

416. Why estimate time and cost?

417. When do the individual activities need to start and finish?

418. What is the total time required to complete the Valuation Advisory project if no delays occur?

419. Done before proceeding with this activity or what can be done concurrently?

420. Small or large Valuation Advisory project?

421. Do any colleagues have experience with your organization and/or RFPs?

2.19 Project Schedule: Valuation Advisory

422. How can you address that situation?

423. How do you know that youhave done this right?

424. How do you manage Valuation Advisory project Risk?

425. Have all Valuation Advisory project delays been adequately accounted for, communicated to all stakeholders and adjustments made in overall Valuation Advisory project schedule?

426. What is risk management?

427. Should you have a test for each code module?

428. Understand the constraints used in preparing the schedule. Are activities connected because logic dictates the order in which others occur?

429. Are procedures defined by which the Valuation Advisory project schedule may be changed?

430. Are there activities that came from a template or previous Valuation Advisory project that are not applicable on this phase of this Valuation Advisory project?

431. Did the Valuation Advisory project come in on schedule?

432. How much slack is available in the Valuation Advisory project?

433. Change management required?

434. How does a Valuation Advisory project get to be a year late ?

435. To what degree is do you feel the entire team was committed to the Valuation Advisory project schedule?

436. Is infrastructure setup part of your Valuation Advisory project?

437. How effectively were issues able to be resolved without impacting the Valuation Advisory project Schedule or Budget?

438. Is there a Schedule Management Plan that establishes the criteria and activities for developing, monitoring and controlling the Valuation Advisory project schedule?

2.20 Cost Management Plan: Valuation Advisory

439. Risk Analysis?

440. Is your organization certified as a broker of the products/supplies?

441. What weaknesses do you have?

442. Will the earned value reporting interface between time and cost management?

443. Are mitigation strategies identified?

444. Has the business need been clearly defined?

445. Are risk triggers captured?

446. Are quality inspections and review activities listed in the Valuation Advisory project schedule(s)?

447. Has a sponsor been identified?

448. Has a quality assurance plan been developed for the Valuation Advisory project?

449. Is it a Valuation Advisory project?

450. How difficult will it be to do specific tasks on the Valuation Advisory project?

451. Have all necessary approvals been obtained?

452. Eac -estimate at completion, what is the total job expected to cost?

453. How does the proposed individual meet each requirement?

454. Are decisions captured in a decisions log?

455. What is cost and Valuation Advisory project cost management?

456. What will be the split of responsibilities of progress measurement and controls among the owner, contractor, subcontractors, and vendors?

2.21 Activity Cost Estimates: Valuation Advisory

457. Who determines the quality and expertise of contractors?

458. Specific - is the objective clear in terms of what, how, when, and where the situation will be changed?

459. Does the activity use a common approach or business function to deliver its results?

460. Certification of actual expenditures?

461. What is included in indirect cost being allocated?

462. What is Valuation Advisory project cost management?

463. Is there anything unique in this Valuation Advisory projects scope statement that will affect resources?

464. How do you change activities?

465. Were the tasks or work products prepared by the consultant useful?

466. Measurable - are the targets measurable?

467. What makes a good activity description?

468. Are data needed on characteristics of care?

469. In which phase of the acquisition process cycle does source qualifications reside?

470. What are the audit requirements?

471. Performance bond should always provide what part of the contract value?

472. How many activities should you have?

473. Vac -variance at completion, how much over/ under budget do you expect to be?

474. How do you do activity recasts?

475. What areas does the group agree are the biggest success on the Valuation Advisory project?

476. Were sponsors and decision makers available when needed outside regularly scheduled meetings?

2.22 Cost Estimating Worksheet: Valuation Advisory

477. Ask: are others positioned to know, are others credible, and will others cooperate?

478. What costs are to be estimated?

479. Is it feasible to establish a control group arrangement?

480. Value pocket identification & quantification what are value pockets?

481. Is the Valuation Advisory project responsive to community need?

482. What can be included?

483. Will the Valuation Advisory project collaborate with the local community and leverage resources?

484. How will the results be shared and to whom?

485. What will others want?

486. Does the Valuation Advisory project provide innovative ways for stakeholders to overcome obstacles or deliver better outcomes?

487. What additional Valuation Advisory project(s) could be initiated as a result of this Valuation Advisory project?

488. Who is best positioned to know and assist in identifying corresponding factors?

489. Can a trend be established from historical performance data on the selected measure and are the criteria for using trend analysis or forecasting methods met?

490. What is the estimated labor cost today based upon this information?

491. What is the purpose of estimating?

492. Identify the timeframe necessary to monitor progress and collect data to determine how the selected measure has changed?

493. What happens to any remaining funds not used?

2.23 Cost Baseline: Valuation Advisory

494. How will cost estimates be used?

495. Are you asking management for something as a result of this update?

496. Has the Valuation Advisory project (or Valuation Advisory project phase) been evaluated against each objective established in the product description and Integrated Valuation Advisory project Plan?

497. Have the lessons learned been filed with the Valuation Advisory project Management Office?

498. Review your risk triggers -have your risks changed?

499. At which frequency ?

500. For what purpose ?

501. What is the reality?

502. Should a more thorough impact analysis be conducted?

503. How do you manage cost?

504. Is request in line with priorities?

505. Has the actual cost of the Valuation Advisory

project (or Valuation Advisory project phase) been tallied and compared to the approved budget?

506. Has operations management formally accepted responsibility for operating and maintaining the product(s) or service(s) delivered by the Valuation Advisory project?

507. Is the requested change request a result of changes in other Valuation Advisory project(s)?

508. Does a process exist for establishing a cost baseline to measure Valuation Advisory project performance?

509. What is cost and Valuation Advisory project cost management?

510. How concrete were original objectives?

511. What do you want to measure ?

512. Does the suggested change request represent a desired enhancement to the products functionality?

2.24 Quality Management Plan: Valuation Advisory

513. Does the program use other agents to collect samples?

514. What are the appropriate test methods to be used?

515. Are formal code reviews conducted?

516. What would be the next steps or what else should you do at this point?

517. How are corresponding standards measured?

518. What has the QM Collaboration done?

519. Checking the completeness and appropriateness of the sampling and testing. Were the right locations/ samples tested for the right parameters?

520. Is it necessary?

521. Who gets results of work?

522. What are your organizations key processes (product, service, business, and support)?

523. Account for the procedures used to verify the data quality of the data being reviewed?

524. How does your organization determine the

requirements and product/service features important to customers?

525. Methodology followed?

526. How is equipment calibrated?

527. Documented results available?

528. Meet how often?

529. Are requirements management tracking tools and procedures in place?

530. How do you measure?

531. Who is responsible?

2.25 Quality Metrics: Valuation Advisory

532. Were number of defects identified?

533. What method of measurement do you use?

534. Are documents on hand to provide explanations of privacy and confidentiality?

535. Are there any open risk issues?

536. How are requirements conflicts resolved?

537. What is the benchmark?

538. Who is willing to lead?

539. How do you calculate corresponding metrics?

540. Have risk areas been identified?

541. How should customers provide input?

542. Has trace of defects been initiated?

543. Was review conducted per standard protocols?

544. Should a modifier be included?

545. How does one achieve stability?

546. How do you communicate results and findings to

upper management?

547. Is quality culture a competitive advantage?

548. When will the Final Guidance will be issued?

549. What forces exist that would cause them to change?

550. What are your organizations expectations for its quality Valuation Advisory project?

2.26 Process Improvement Plan: Valuation Advisory

551. If a process improvement framework is being used, which elements will help the problems and goals listed?

552. Are there forms and procedures to collect and record the data?

553. What personnel are the coaches for your initiative?

554. What is the return on investment?

555. Are you making progress on the improvement framework?

556. Why do you want to achieve the goal?

557. Where do you focus?

558. Has the time line required to move measurement results from the points of collection to databases or users been established?

559. Where are you now?

560. What personnel are the change agents for your initiative?

561. What lessons have you learned so far?

562. Modeling current processes is great, and will you ever see a return on that investment?

563. What is quality and how will you ensure it?

564. Purpose of goal: the motive is determined by asking, why do you want to achieve this goal?

565. Management commitment at all levels?

566. Has a process guide to collect the data been developed?

567. Does your process ensure quality?

568. What personnel are the sponsors for that initiative?

569. What is the test-cycle concept?

570. Have storage and access mechanisms and procedures been determined?

2.27 Responsibility Assignment Matrix: Valuation Advisory

571. Changes in the overhead pool and/or organization structures?

572. What is the number one predictor of a groups productivity?

573. What happens when others get pulled for higher priority Valuation Advisory projects?

574. Time-phased control account budgets?

575. With too many people labeled as doing the work, are there too many hands involved?

576. Is every signing-off responsibility and every communicating responsibility critically necessary?

577. How many hours by each staff member/rate?

578. Does a missing responsibility indicate that the current Valuation Advisory project is not yet fully understood?

579. Budgets assigned to major functional organizations?

580. Changes in the nature of the overhead requirements?

581. Is accountability placed at the lowest-possible

level within the Valuation Advisory project so that decisions can be made at that level?

582. What do you do when people do not respond?

583. Evaluate the impact of schedule changes, work around, etc?

584. Are people encouraged to bring up issues?

585. Cwbs elements to be subcontracted, with identification of subcontractors?

586. What is the justification?

587. Does the contractors system identify work accomplishment against the schedule plan?

588. Does each activity-deliverable have exactly one Accountable responsibility, so that accountability is clear and decisions can be made quickly?

2.28 Roles and Responsibilities: Valuation Advisory

589. What areas of supervision are challenging for you?

590. What are your major roles and responsibilities in the area of performance measurement and assessment?

591. What specific behaviors did you observe?

592. Are Valuation Advisory project team roles and responsibilities identified and documented?

593. Concern: where are you limited or have no authority, where you can not influence?

594. Are Valuation Advisory project team roles and responsibilities identified and documented?

595. Was the expectation clearly communicated?

596. Is feedback clearly communicated and non-judgmental?

597. Are your policies supportive of a culture of quality data?

598. Do you take the time to clearly define roles and responsibilities on Valuation Advisory project tasks?

599. Influence: what areas of organizational decision

making are you able to influence when you do not have authority to make the final decision?

600. What should you highlight for improvement?

601. Are the quality assurance functions and related roles and responsibilities clearly defined?

602. How is your work-life balance?

603. Key conclusions and recommendations: Are conclusions and recommendations relevant and acceptable?

604. What is working well?

605. Is there a training program in place for stakeholders covering expectations, roles and responsibilities and any addition knowledge others need to be good stakeholders?

606. Be specific; avoid generalities. Thank you and great work alone are insufficient. What exactly do you appreciate and why?

607. What expectations were NOT met?

608. What should you do now to ensure that you are exceeding expectations and excelling in your current position?

2.29 Human Resource Management Plan: Valuation Advisory

609. Are key risk mitigation strategies added to the Valuation Advisory project schedule?

610. Are tasks tracked by hours?

611. Are target dates established for each milestone deliverable?

612. Are written status reports provided on a designated frequent basis?

613. Have all involved Valuation Advisory project stakeholders and work groups committed to the Valuation Advisory project?

614. Are internal Valuation Advisory project status meetings held at reasonable intervals?

615. Is your organization certified as a supplier, wholesaler, regular dealer, or manufacturer of corresponding products/supplies?

616. Does the resource management plan include a personnel development plan?

617. Are all vendor contracts closed out?

618. Account for the purpose of this Valuation Advisory project by describing, at a high-level, what will be done. What is this Valuation Advisory project

aiming to achieve?

619. Are estimating assumptions and constraints captured?

620. Did the Valuation Advisory project team have the right skills?

621. Are post milestone Valuation Advisory project reviews (PMPR) conducted with your organization at least once a year?

622. Are assumptions being identified, recorded, analyzed, qualified and closed?

623. Has the scope management document been updated and distributed to help prevent scope creep?

624. Is there a formal set of procedures supporting Stakeholder Management?

625. Are changes in scope (deliverable commitments) agreed to by all affected groups & individuals?

2.30 Communications Management Plan: Valuation Advisory

626. What communications method?

627. What approaches do you use?

628. Are there potential barriers between the team and the stakeholder?

629. What steps can you take for a positive relationship?

630. What approaches to you feel are the best ones to use?

631. How is this initiative related to other portfolios, programs, or Valuation Advisory projects?

632. Can you think of other people who might have concerns or interests?

633. Are the stakeholders getting the information others need, are others consulted, are concerns addressed?

634. Do you feel a register helps?

635. Do you feel more overwhelmed by stakeholders?

636. Are there too many who have an interest in some aspect of your work?

637. What are the interrelationships?

638. How did the term stakeholder originate?

639. Who are the members of the governing body?

640. Are others part of the communications management plan?

641. Conflict resolution -which method when?

642. What is the political influence?

643. Who have you worked with in past, similar initiatives?

644. What help do you and your team need from the stakeholder?

645. How will the person responsible for executing the communication item be notified?

2.31 Risk Management Plan: Valuation Advisory

646. Can the risk be avoided by choosing a different alternative?

647. What are the chances the event will occur?

648. What would you do?

649. Do the people have the right combinations of skills?

650. Is a software Valuation Advisory project management tool available?

651. Could others have been better mitigated?

652. Is the customer willing to commit significant time to the requirements gathering process?

653. What risks are tracked?

654. Is there additional information that would make you more confident about your analysis?

655. How risk averse are you?

656. Can you stabilize dynamic risk factors?

657. Risk probability and impact: how will the probabilities and impacts of risk items be assessed?

658. What is the cost to the Valuation Advisory project if it does occur?

659. Is the process supported by tools?

660. Are people attending meetings and doing work?

661. How is risk monitoring performed?

662. Have staff received necessary training?

663. Are status updates being made on schedule and are the updates clearly described?

664. Are formal technical reviews part of this process?

665. How quickly does this item need to be resolved?

2.32 Risk Register: Valuation Advisory

666. How are risks identified?

667. How is a Community Risk Register created?

668. What has changed since the last period?

669. What will be done?

670. Risk categories: what are the main categories of risks that should be addressed on this Valuation Advisory project?

671. Financial risk -can your organization afford to undertake the Valuation Advisory project?

672. Which key risks have ineffective responses or outstanding improvement actions?

673. Can the likelihood and impact of failing to achieve corresponding recommendations and action plans be assessed?

674. How are risks graded?

675. Are corrective measures implemented as planned?

676. What is a Community Risk Register?

677. Are your objectives at risk?

678. Amongst the action plans and recommendations

that you have to introduce are there some that could stop or delay the overall program?

679. What is your current and future risk profile?

680. What is a Risk?

681. Recovery actions - planned actions taken once a risk has occurred to allow you to move on. What should you do after?

682. What could prevent you delivering on the strategic program objectives and what is being done to mitigate corresponding issues?

683. When would you develop a risk register?

684. What is the appropriate level of risk management for this Valuation Advisory project?

2.33 Probability and Impact Assessment: Valuation Advisory

685. What new technologies are being explored in the same area?

686. Risk data quality assessment - what is the quality of the data used to determine or assess the risk?

687. Have you worked with the customer in the past?

688. Does the Valuation Advisory project team have experience with the technology to be implemented?

689. What is the likelihood?

690. Do the requirements require the creation of new algorithms?

691. What can you do about it?

692. Is the Valuation Advisory project cutting across the entire organization?

693. What is the likelihood of a breakthrough?

694. Do you manage the process through use of metrics?

695. What is the level of experience available with your organization?

696. What will be cost of redeployment of personnel?

697. My Valuation Advisory project leader has suddenly left your organization, what do you do?

698. Will there be an increase in the political conservatism?

699. How carefully have the potential competitors been identified?

700. What things might go wrong?

701. Are tools for analysis and design available?

702. Which of corresponding risk factors can be avoided altogether?

703. What is the risk appetite?

2.34 Probability and Impact Matrix: Valuation Advisory

704. Are team members trained in the use of the tools?

705. Which phase of the Valuation Advisory project do you take part in?

706. During Valuation Advisory project executing, a team member identifies a risk that is not in the risk register. What should you do?

707. Were there any Valuation Advisory projects similar to this one in existence?

708. Brain storm – mind maps, what if?

709. How completely has the customer been identified?

710. What are its business ethics?

711. What things are likely to change?

712. How much is the probability of the risk occurring?

713. Can the Valuation Advisory project proceed without assuming the risk?

714. Is the delay in one subValuation Advisory project going to affect another?

715. Has the need for the Valuation Advisory project been properly established?

716. Do end-users have realistic expectations?

717. Premium on reliability of product?

718. What is Valuation Advisory project risk management?

719. Mandated delivery date?

720. Is Valuation Advisory project scope stable?

721. Pay attention to the quality of the plans: is the content complete, or does it seem to be lacking detail?

2.35 Risk Data Sheet: Valuation Advisory

722. How do you handle product safely?

723. What was measured?

724. Who has a vested interest in how you perform as your organization (our stakeholders)?

725. Are new hazards created?

726. What is the duration of infection (the length of time the host is infected with the organizm) in a normal healthy human host?

727. Type of risk identified?

728. What are the main threats to your existence?

729. What can you do?

730. What is the environment within which you operate (social trends, economic, community values, broad based participation, national directions etc.)?

731. Has a sensitivity analysis been carried out?

732. What are you trying to achieve (Objectives)?

733. What are you weak at and therefore need to do better?

734. If it happens, what are the consequences?

735. How reliable is the data source?

736. Whom do you serve (customers)?

737. How can hazards be reduced?

738. What were the Causes that contributed?

739. What will be the consequences if it happens?

740. What actions can be taken to eliminate or remove risk?

741. What if client refuses?

2.36 Procurement Management Plan: Valuation Advisory

742. Is there a set of procedures defining the scope, procedures, and deliverables defining quality control?

743. Are the quality tools and methods identified in the Quality Plan appropriate to the Valuation Advisory project?

744. Is the Valuation Advisory project sponsor clearly communicating the business case or rationale for why this Valuation Advisory project is needed?

745. Is there an onboarding process in place?

746. Is Valuation Advisory project work proceeding in accordance with the original Valuation Advisory project schedule?

747. Does the schedule include Valuation Advisory project management time and change request analysis time?

748. Are adequate resources provided for the quality assurance function?

749. Are the results of quality assurance reviews provided to affected groups & individuals?

750. Is the schedule updated on a periodic basis?

751. Are action items captured and managed?

752. Are milestone deliverables effectively tracked and compared to Valuation Advisory project plan?

753. Are parking lot items captured?

754. Does the Valuation Advisory project have a Quality Culture?

755. Are Valuation Advisory project leaders committed to this Valuation Advisory project full time?

756. Have all involved Valuation Advisory project stakeholders and work groups committed to the Valuation Advisory project?

757. Are non-critical path items updated and agreed upon with the teams?

2.37 Source Selection Criteria: Valuation Advisory

758. When is it appropriate to issue a Draft Request for Proposal (DRFP)?

759. What should be considered when developing evaluation standards?

760. How will you evaluate offerors proposals?

761. How long will it take for the purchase cost to be the same as the lease cost?

762. What documentation should be used to support the selection decision?

763. What source selection software is your team using?

764. Which contract type places the most risk on the seller?

765. What should clarifications include?

766. Has all proposal data been loaded?

767. What should a DRFP include?

768. How do you encourage efficiency and consistency?

769. What procedures are followed when a contractor

requires access to classified information or a significant quantity of special material/information?

770. What instructions should be provided regarding oral presentations?

771. How should comments received in response to a RFP be handled?

772. Are they compliant with all technical requirements?

773. Are resultant proposal revisions allowed?

774. When and what information can be considered with offerors regarding past performance?

775. What are the guiding principles for developing an evaluation report?

776. How can the methods of publicizing the buy be tailored to yield more effective price competition?

777. What documentation is needed for a tradeoff decision?

2.38 Stakeholder Management Plan: Valuation Advisory

778. Detail warranty and/or maintenance periods?

779. Are changes in deliverable commitments agreed to by all affected groups & individuals?

780. How many Valuation Advisory project staff does this specific process affect?

781. What guidelines or procedures currently exist that must be adhered to (eg departmental accounting procedures)?

782. Is the Valuation Advisory project sponsor clearly communicating the business case or rationale for why this Valuation Advisory project is needed?

783. Is Valuation Advisory project status reviewed with the steering and executive teams at appropriate intervals?

784. How accurate and complete is the information?

785. Is the performance of the supplier to be rated and documented?

786. Were Valuation Advisory project team members involved in the development of activity & task decomposition?

787. Have Valuation Advisory project team

accountabilities & responsibilities been clearly defined?

788. Are the Valuation Advisory project team members located locally to the users/stakeholders?

789. Have process improvement efforts been completed before requirements efforts begin?

790. Is a pmo (Valuation Advisory project management office) in place and does it provide oversight to the Valuation Advisory project?

2.39 Change Management Plan: Valuation Advisory

791. What is the most positive interpretation it can receive?

792. Has the priority for this Valuation Advisory project been set by the Business Unit Management Team?

793. What would be an estimate of the total cost for the activities required to carry out the change initiative?

794. What are the major changes to processes?

795. What goal(s) do you hope to accomplish?

796. Is there a software application relevant to this deliverable?

797. What is the negative impact of communicating too soon or too late?

798. Who will do the training?

799. What skills, education, knowledge, or work experiences should the resources have for each identified competency?

800. Why is the initiative is being undertaken - What are the business drivers?

801. Has an information & communications plan been developed?

802. Where will the funds come from?

803. Have the approved procedures and policies been published?

804. How does the principle of senders and receivers make the Valuation Advisory project communications effort more complex?

805. How can you best frame the message so that it addresses the audiences interests?

806. What roles within your organization are affected, and how?

807. Who might be able to help you the most?

808. What will be the preferred method of delivery?

809. How badly can information be misinterpreted?

810. How will you deal with anger about the restricting of communications due to confidentiality considerations?

3.0 Executing Process Group: Valuation Advisory

811. Based on your Valuation Advisory project communication management plan, what worked well?

812. What are the key components of the Valuation Advisory project communications plan?

813. What factors are contributing to progress or delay in the achievement of products and results?

814. After how many days will the lease cost be the same as the purchase cost for the equipment?

815. How many different communication channels does the Valuation Advisory project team have?

816. What is the shortest possible time it will take to complete this Valuation Advisory project?

817. What are the typical Valuation Advisory project management skills?

818. How well did the team follow the chosen processes?

819. What does it mean to take a systems view of a Valuation Advisory project?

820. Are decisions made in a timely manner?

821. What is involved in the solicitation process?

822. Does the case present a realistic scenario?

823. What are the critical steps involved with strategy mapping?

824. Who are the Valuation Advisory project stakeholders?

825. If action is called for, what form should it take?

826. What are the main processes included in Valuation Advisory project quality management?

827. Do the partners have sufficient financial capacity to keep up the benefits produced by the programme?

828. Is the Valuation Advisory project making progress in helping to achieve the set results?

829. What are the critical steps involved in selecting measures and initiatives?

3.1 Team Member Status Report: Valuation Advisory

830. Is there evidence that staff is taking a more professional approach toward management of your organizations Valuation Advisory projects?

831. How does this product, good, or service meet the needs of the Valuation Advisory project and your organization as a whole?

832. Will the staff do training or is that done by a third party?

833. Are the attitudes of staff regarding Valuation Advisory project work improving?

834. Do you have an Enterprise Valuation Advisory project Management Office (EPMO)?

835. How much risk is involved?

836. Why is it to be done?

837. How will resource planning be done?

838. When a teams productivity and success depend on collaboration and the efficient flow of information, what generally fails them?

839. Are your organizations Valuation Advisory projects more successful over time?

840. Does your organization have the means (staff, money, contract, etc.) to produce or to acquire the product, good, or service?

841. How can you make it practical?

842. What specific interest groups do you have in place?

843. What is to be done?

844. The problem with Reward & Recognition Programs is that the truly deserving people all too often get left out. How can you make it practical?

845. Does every department have to have a Valuation Advisory project Manager on staff?

846. Are the products of your organizations Valuation Advisory projects meeting customers objectives?

847. Does the product, good, or service already exist within your organization?

848. How it is to be done?

3.2 Change Request: Valuation Advisory

849. What mechanism is used to appraise others of changes that are made?

850. What needs to be communicated?

851. What is the relationship between requirements attributes and reliability?

852. Are change requests logged and managed?

853. What are the duties of the change control team?

854. How fast will change requests be approved?

855. Who needs to approve change requests?

856. Who is communicating the change?

857. Is it feasible to use requirements attributes as predictors of reliability?

858. How can changes be graded?

859. Have all related configuration items been properly updated?

860. For which areas does this operating procedure apply?

861. What must be taken into consideration when

introducing change control programs?

862. Who is included in the change control team?

863. Where do changes come from?

864. What are the basic mechanics of the Change Advisory Board (CAB)?

865. What is the function of the change control committee?

866. How is the change documented (format, content, storage)?

867. Who is responsible to authorize changes?

3.3 Change Log: Valuation Advisory

868. Do the described changes impact on the integrity or security of the system?

869. Is the requested change request a result of changes in other Valuation Advisory project(s)?

870. Does the suggested change request seem to represent a necessary enhancement to the product?

871. Is this a mandatory replacement?

872. Is the submitted change a new change or a modification of a previously approved change?

873. Who initiated the change request?

874. How does this change affect the timeline of the schedule?

875. Is the change request within Valuation Advisory project scope?

876. When was the request submitted?

877. Is the change request open, closed or pending?

878. When was the request approved?

879. Is the change backward compatible without limitations?

880. How does this relate to the standards developed

for specific business processes?

881. Will the Valuation Advisory project fail if the change request is not executed?

882. How does this change affect scope?

3.4 Decision Log: Valuation Advisory

883. How does an increasing emphasis on cost containment influence the strategies and tactics used?

884. How do you define success?

885. Does anything need to be adjusted?

886. How do you know when you are achieving it?

887. With whom was the decision shared or considered?

888. What is your overall strategy for quality control / quality assurance procedures?

889. What eDiscovery problem or issue did your organization set out to fix or make better?

890. Is your opponent open to a non-traditional workflow, or will it likely challenge anything you do?

891. How consolidated and comprehensive a story can you tell by capturing currently available incident data in a central location and through a log of key decisions during an incident?

892. What alternatives/risks were considered?

893. At what point in time does loss become unacceptable?

894. It becomes critical to track and periodically revisit both operational effectiveness; Are you noticing all that you need to, and are you interpreting what you see effectively?

895. Do strategies and tactics aimed at less than full control reduce the costs of management or simply shift the cost burden?

896. Is everything working as expected?

897. Who will be given a copy of this document and where will it be kept?

898. What are the cost implications?

899. Which variables make a critical difference?

900. What makes you different or better than others companies selling the same thing?

901. What is the average size of your matters in an applicable measurement?

902. Linked to original objective?

3.5 Quality Audit: Valuation Advisory

903. Is the continuing professional education of key personnel account fored in detail?

904. Are all records associated with the reconditioning of a device maintained for a minimum of two years after the sale or disposal of the last device within a lot of merchandise?

905. How does your organization know that its staff financial services are appropriately effective and constructive?

906. Are all employees made aware of device defects which may occur from the improper performance of specific jobs?

907. How does your organization know that its system for managing intellectual property issues is appropriately effective, constructive and fair?

908. How does your organization know that the range and quality of its accommodation, catering and transportation services are appropriately effective and constructive?

909. Does everyone know what they are supposed to be doing, how and why?

910. How does the organization know that its system for maintaining and advancing the capabilities of its staff, particularly in relation to the Mission of the organization, is appropriately effective and

constructive?

911. What happens if your organization fails its Quality Audit?

912. Do the acceptance procedures and specifications include the criteria for acceptance/rejection, define the process to be used, and specify the measuring and test equipment that is to be used?

913. Are complaint files maintained?

914. Has a written procedure been established to identify devices during all stages of receipt, reconditioning, distribution and installation so that mix-ups are prevented?

915. How does your organization know that the review processes are effective?

916. Does the suppliers quality system have a written procedure for corrective action when a defect occurs?

917. For each device to be reconditioned, are device specifications, such as appropriate engineering drawings, component specifications and software specifications, maintained?

918. How does your organization know that its Mission, Vision and Values Statements are appropriate and effectively guiding your organization?

919. How does your organization know that its relationship with its (past) staff is appropriately effective and constructive?

920. Is there a written procedure for receiving materials?

921. How does your organization know that its system for attending to the particular needs of its international staff is appropriately effective and constructive?

922. How does your organization know that the quality of its supervisors is appropriately effective and constructive?

3.6 Team Directory: Valuation Advisory

923. Decisions: is the most suitable form of contract being used?

924. Who will be the stakeholders on your next Valuation Advisory project?

925. Decisions: what could be done better to improve the quality of the constructed product?

926. What are you going to deliver or accomplish?

927. How does the team resolve conflicts and ensure tasks are completed?

928. Process decisions: are there any statutory or regulatory issues relevant to the timely execution of work?

929. Who are the Team Members?

930. Process decisions: is work progressing on schedule and per contract requirements?

931. How will the team handle changes?

932. Who will talk to the customer?

933. Where will the product be used and/or delivered or built when appropriate?

934. When does information need to be distributed?

935. Do purchase specifications and configurations match requirements?

936. Does a Valuation Advisory project team directory list all resources assigned to the Valuation Advisory project?

937. Have you decided when to celebrate the Valuation Advisory projects completion date?

938. Process decisions: are contractors adequately prosecuting the work?

939. Process decisions: do job conditions warrant additional actions to collect job information and document on-site activity?

940. Who will report Valuation Advisory project status to all stakeholders?

941. Who should receive information (all stakeholders)?

3.7 Team Operating Agreement: Valuation Advisory

942. What are some potential sources of conflict among team members?

943. How will your group handle planned absences?

944. How will you resolve conflict efficiently and respectfully?

945. Confidentiality: how will confidential information be handled?

946. What are the current caseload numbers in the unit?

947. Are there more than two national cultures represented by your team?

948. Do you leverage technology engagement tools group chat, polls, screen sharing, etc.?

949. Do you brief absent members after they view meeting notes or listen to a recording?

950. Do you call or email participants to ensure understanding, follow-through and commitment to the meeting outcomes?

951. The method to be used in the decision making process; Will it be consensus, majority rule, or the supervisor having the final say?

952. Do you listen for voice tone and word choice to understand the meaning behind words?

953. Methodologies: how will key team processes be implemented, such as training, research, work deliverable production, review and approval processes, knowledge management, and meeting procedures?

954. Do you determine the meeting length and time of day?

955. Have you set the goals and objectives of the team?

956. How will group handle unplanned absences?

957. Do you solicit member feedback about meetings and what would make them better?

958. Has the appropriate access to relevant data and analysis capability been granted?

959. Are there differences in access to communication and collaboration technology based on team member location?

960. Do you use a parking lot for any items that are important and outside of the agenda?

961. How do you want to be thought of and known within your organization?

3.8 Team Performance Assessment: Valuation Advisory

962. To what degree does the teams purpose constitute a broader, deeper aspiration than just accomplishing short-term goals?

963. To what degree will the team ensure that all members equitably share the work essential to the success of the team?

964. What structural changes have you made or are you preparing to make?

965. Social categorization and intergroup behaviour: Does minimal intergroup discrimination make social identity more positive?

966. To what degree are sub-teams possible or necessary?

967. To what degree are the skill areas critical to team performance present?

968. To what degree can team members frequently and easily communicate with one another?

969. Do friends perform better than acquaintances?

970. To what degree does the teams approach to its work allow for modification and improvement over time?

971. To what degree do all members feel responsible for all agreed-upon measures?

972. When does the medium matter?

973. How do you encourage members to learn from each other?

974. To what degree can all members engage in open and interactive considerations?

975. To what degree will the approach capitalize on and enhance the skills of all team members in a manner that takes into consideration other demands on members of the team?

976. To what degree are the goals ambitious?

977. To what degree do team members articulate the teams work approach?

978. To what degree do team members agree with the goals, relative importance, and the ways in which achievement will be measured?

979. To what degree will the team adopt a concrete, clearly understood, and agreed-upon approach that will result in achievement of the teams goals?

980. To what degree does the teams work approach provide opportunity for members to engage in fact-based problem solving?

981. How do you manage human resources?

3.9 Team Member Performance Assessment: Valuation Advisory

982. How do you currently account for your results in the teams achievement?

983. Are any validation activities performed?

984. How effective is training that is delivered through technology-based platforms?

985. Who they are?

986. How is performance assessment used in making future award decisions including options and extend/compete decisions?

987. Is it clear how goals will be accomplished?

988. What are the staffs preferences for training on technology-based platforms?

989. What resources do you need?

990. To what degree do team members understand one anothers roles and skills?

991. To what degree are the goals realistic?

992. How are assessments designed, delivered, and otherwise used to maximize training?

993. Verify business objectives. Are they appropriate,

and well-articulated?

994. To what degree does the teams purpose contain themes that are particularly meaningful and memorable?

995. What makes them effective?

996. To what degree does the team possess adequate membership to achieve its ends?

997. Why do performance reviews?

3.10 Issue Log: Valuation Advisory

998. Who is involved as you identify stakeholders?

999. Is the issue log kept in a safe place?

1000. How do you reply to this question; you am new here and managing this major program. How do you suggest you build your network?

1001. Which stakeholders can influence others?

1002. What steps can you take for positive relationships?

1003. Why do you manage communications?

1004. In your work, how much time is spent on stakeholder identification?

1005. What help do you and your team need from the stakeholders?

1006. What are the stakeholders interrelationships?

1007. Do you often overlook a key stakeholder or stakeholder group?

1008. What is a Stakeholder?

1009. What are the typical contents?

1010. Why do you manage human resources?

1011. Where do team members get information?

1012. How often do you engage with stakeholders?

1013. Why multiple evaluators?

4.0 Monitoring and Controlling Process Group: Valuation Advisory

1014. What business situation is being addressed?

1015. How to ensure validity, quality and consistency?

1016. If a risk event occurs, what will you do?

1017. What were things that you need to improve?

1018. What were things that you did well, and could improve, and how?

1019. How well did you do?

1020. How can you monitor progress?

1021. Feasibility: how much money, time, and effort can you put into this?

1022. Were decisions made in a timely manner?

1023. What do they need to know about the Valuation Advisory project?

1024. How will staff learn how to use the deliverables?

1025. What will you do to minimize the impact should a risk event occur?

1026. Key stakeholders to work with. How many potential communications channels exist on the

Valuation Advisory project?

1027. Is there sufficient funding available for this?

4.1 Project Performance Report: Valuation Advisory

1028. To what degree do the relationships of the informal organization motivate taskrelevant behavior and facilitate task completion?

1029. To what degree will each member have the opportunity to advance his or her professional skills in all three of the above categories while contributing to the accomplishment of the teams purpose and goals?

1030. To what degree are the teams goals and objectives clear, simple, and measurable?

1031. To what degree do the goals specify concrete team work products?

1032. To what degree can the team measure progress against specific goals?

1033. To what degree does the information network provide individuals with the information they require?

1034. To what degree can team members vigorously define the teams purpose in considerations with others who are not part of the functioning team?

1035. What is the degree to which rules govern information exchange between groups?

1036. To what degree do individual skills and abilities match task demands?

1037. To what degree are fresh input and perspectives systematically caught and added (for example, through information and analysis, new members, and senior sponsors)?

1038. What is in it for you?

1039. What degree are the relative importance and priority of the goals clear to all team members?

1040. To what degree are the members clear on what they are individually responsible for and what they are jointly responsible for?

4.2 Variance Analysis: Valuation Advisory

1041. There are detailed schedules which support control account and work package start and completion dates/events?

1042. Does the contractors system provide unit or lot costs when applicable?

1043. Favorable or unfavorable variance?

1044. Who is generally responsible for monitoring and taking action on variances?

1045. What is the total budget for the Valuation Advisory project (including estimates for authorized and unpriced work)?

1046. Are all cwbs elements specified for external reporting?

1047. How do you haverify authorization to proceed with all authorized work?

1048. Do work packages consist of discrete tasks which are adequately described?

1049. Are the bases and rates for allocating costs from each indirect pool consistently applied?

1050. Are detailed work packages planned as far in advance as practicable?

1051. At what point should variances be isolated and brought to the attention of the management?

1052. Are authorized changes being incorporated in a timely manner?

1053. Do the rates and prices remain constant throughout the year?

1054. What types of services and expense are shared between business segments?

1055. Are significant decision points, constraints, and interfaces identified as key milestones?

1056. What business event causes fluctuations?

1057. Are all budgets assigned to control accounts?

1058. What costs are avoidable if one or more customers are dropped?

1059. Is budgeted cost for work performed calculated in a manner consistent with the way work is planned?

1060. How do you identify and isolate causes of favorable and unfavorable cost and schedule variances?

4.3 Earned Value Status: Valuation Advisory

1061. Where are your problem areas?

1062. What is the unit of forecast value?

1063. How does this compare with other Valuation Advisory projects?

1064. If earned value management (EVM) is so good in determining the true status of a Valuation Advisory project and Valuation Advisory project its completion, why is it that hardly any one uses it in information systems related Valuation Advisory projects?

1065. Earned value can be used in almost any Valuation Advisory project situation and in almost any Valuation Advisory project environment. it may be used on large Valuation Advisory projects, medium sized Valuation Advisory projects, tiny Valuation Advisory projects (in cut-down form), complex and simple Valuation Advisory projects and in any market sector. some people, of course, know all about earned value, they have used it for years - but perhaps not as effectively as they could have?

1066. When is it going to finish?

1067. Where is evidence-based earned value in your organization reported?

1068. Validation is a process of ensuring that

the developed system will actually achieve the stakeholders desired outcomes; Are you building the right product? What do you validate?

1069. Verification is a process of ensuring that the developed system satisfies the stakeholders agreements and specifications; Are you building the product right? What do you haverify?

1070. How much is it going to cost by the finish?

1071. Are you hitting your Valuation Advisory projects targets?

4.4 Risk Audit: Valuation Advisory

1072. Are the software tools integrated with each other?

1073. Have all involved been advised of any obligations they have to sponsors?

1074. Will participants be required to sign a legally counselled waiver or risk disclaimer when entering an event?

1075. Is the auditor able to evaluate contradictory evidence in an unbiased manner?

1076. Is the customer technically sophisticated in the product area?

1077. Are corresponding safety and risk management policies posted for all to see?

1078. Is there a screening process that will ensure all participants have the fitness and skills required to safely participate?

1079. Are risk management strategies documented?

1080. Do requirements demand the use of new analysis, design, or testing methods?

1081. What impact does experience with one client have on decisions made for other clients during the risk-assessment process?

1082. Is all required equipment available?

1083. Are policies communicated to all affected?

1084. Does the customer understand the process?

1085. To what extent are auditors influenced by the business risk assessment in the audit process, and how can auditors create more effective mental models to more fully examine contradictory evidence?

1086. Do you have financial policies and procedures in place to guide officers of your organization/treasurer/ general members?

1087. What are risks and how do you manage them?

1088. To what extent should analytical procedures be utilized in the risk-assessment process?

1089. Do you have a clear plan for the future that describes what you want to do and how you are going to do it?

1090. Does the adoption of a business risk audit approach change internal control documentation and testing practices?

4.5 Contractor Status Report: Valuation Advisory

1091. What was the final actual cost?

1092. How long have you been using the services?

1093. What process manages the contracts?

1094. What was the overall budget or estimated cost?

1095. What is the average response time for answering a support call?

1096. Describe how often regular updates are made to the proposed solution. Are corresponding regular updates included in the standard maintenance plan?

1097. How is risk transferred?

1098. If applicable; describe your standard schedule for new software version releases. Are new software version releases included in the standard maintenance plan?

1099. What was the budget or estimated cost for your organizations services?

1100. Are there contractual transfer concerns?

1101. What are the minimum and optimal bandwidth requirements for the proposed soluiton?

1102. What was the actual budget or estimated cost for your organizations services?

1103. Who can list a Valuation Advisory project as organization experience, your organization or a previous employee of your organization?

4.6 Formal Acceptance: Valuation Advisory

1104. Was the Valuation Advisory project managed well?

1105. Who supplies data?

1106. Have all comments been addressed?

1107. Was the Valuation Advisory project goal achieved?

1108. Did the Valuation Advisory project achieve its MOV?

1109. Does it do what Valuation Advisory project team said it would?

1110. Is formal acceptance of the Valuation Advisory project product documented and distributed?

1111. What is the Acceptance Management Process?

1112. Do you buy-in installation services?

1113. What features, practices, and processes proved to be strengths or weaknesses?

1114. Does it do what client said it would?

1115. How well did the team follow the methodology?

1116. Was the Valuation Advisory project work done on time, within budget, and according to specification?

1117. Do you perform formal acceptance or burn-in tests?

1118. What lessons were learned about your Valuation Advisory project management methodology?

1119. Do you buy pre-configured systems or build your own configuration?

1120. Was business value realized?

1121. What was done right?

1122. What can you do better next time?

1123. Was the client satisfied with the Valuation Advisory project results?

5.0 Closing Process Group: Valuation Advisory

1124. Did the Valuation Advisory project management methodology work?

1125. Did you do what you said you were going to do?

1126. Who are the Valuation Advisory project stakeholders?

1127. When will the Valuation Advisory project be done?

1128. Is this a follow-on to a previous Valuation Advisory project?

1129. What areas does the group agree are the biggest success on the Valuation Advisory project?

1130. Were cost budgets met?

1131. What communication items need improvement?

1132. What can you do better next time, and what specific actions can you take to improve?

1133. What do you need to do?

1134. Was the schedule met?

1135. How well defined and documented were the

Valuation Advisory project management processes you chose to use?

1136. Did the delivered product meet the specified requirements and goals of the Valuation Advisory project?

1137. How critical is the Valuation Advisory project success to the success of your organization?

1138. Was the user/client satisfied with the end product?

1139. Did you do things well?

5.1 Procurement Audit: Valuation Advisory

1140. Are all complaints of late or incorrect payment sent to a person independent of the already stated having cash disbursement responsibilities?

1141. Are all initial purchase contracts made by the purchasing organization?

1142. Are the rules for automatic payment in computer programs approved by management prior to implementation?

1143. Were the tender documents comprehensive, transparent and free from restrictions or conditions which would discriminate against certain suppliers?

1144. Does the procurement process compile basic procurement information such as how much is bought and spend with individual suppliers?

1145. Was the award criterion only the most economical advantageous tender?

1146. Are procurement policies and practices in line with (international) good practice standards?

1147. Where required, did candidates give evidence of complying with quality assurance standards?

1148. Does your organization have a purchasing policy ?

1149. Are the users needs clearly and invariably defined and has the expected outcome or mission been clearly identified and communicated in measurable terms?

1150. Do procurement staff, supplier and end user communicate properly?

1151. Has the department identified and described the different elements in the procurement process?

1152. Are obtained prices/qualities competitive to prices/qualities obtained by other procurement functions/units, comparing obtained or improved value for money?

1153. Are existing suppliers that have a special right to be consulted being contacted?

1154. Are unusual uses of organization funds investigated?

1155. Are there systems for recording and managing stocks (where part of contract)?

1156. Are the responsibilities for monitoring the execution and performance of contracts clearly assigned?

1157. Is each copy of the purchase order necessary?

1158. Is there a formal program of inservice training for personnel in the business management function?

1159. Are all purchase orders cancelled after payment

to avoid duplicate payment of the same invoice?

5.2 Contract Close-Out: Valuation Advisory

1160. Was the contract type appropriate?

1161. Are the signers the authorized officials?

1162. Has each contract been audited to verify acceptance and delivery?

1163. Was the contract sufficiently clear so as not to result in numerous disputes and misunderstandings?

1164. Parties: who is involved?

1165. Have all contract records been included in the Valuation Advisory project archives?

1166. Change in knowledge?

1167. Change in attitude or behavior?

1168. Parties: Authorized?

1169. Change in circumstances?

1170. What happens to the recipient of services?

1171. How/when used ?

1172. Have all contracts been closed?

1173. Have all acceptance criteria been met prior to

final payment to contractors?

1174. Why Outsource?

1175. How does it work?

1176. Was the contract complete without requiring numerous changes and revisions?

1177. How is the contracting office notified of the automatic contract close-out?

1178. Have all contracts been completed?

1179. What is capture management?

5.3 Project or Phase Close-Out: Valuation Advisory

1180. Can the lesson learned be replicated?

1181. Is the lesson based on actual Valuation Advisory project experience rather than on independent research?

1182. Did the delivered product meet the specified requirements and goals of the Valuation Advisory project?

1183. What were the actual outcomes?

1184. If you were the Valuation Advisory project sponsor, how would you determine which Valuation Advisory project team(s) and/or individuals deserve recognition?

1185. What hierarchical authority does the stakeholder have in your organization?

1186. What was the preferred delivery mechanism?

1187. Planned completion date?

1188. What was expected from each stakeholder?

1189. Were risks identified and mitigated?

1190. What is this stakeholder expecting?

1191. What process was planned for managing issues/ risks?

1192. Planned remaining costs?

1193. What information did each stakeholder need to contribute to the Valuation Advisory projects success?

1194. What were the goals and objectives of the communications strategy for the Valuation Advisory project?

1195. What are the marketing communication needs for each stakeholder?

1196. Who is responsible for award close-out?

1197. What were the desired outcomes?

1198. What could be done to improve the process?

1199. Who controlled key decisions that were made?

5.4 Lessons Learned: Valuation Advisory

1200. Were the Valuation Advisory project objectives met (if not, briefly account for what wasnt met)?

1201. How effective was the documentation that you received with the Valuation Advisory project product/ service?

1202. Did the delivered product meet the specified requirements and goals of the Valuation Advisory project?

1203. How useful and complete was the Valuation Advisory project document repository?

1204. How well were Valuation Advisory project issues communicated throughout your involvement in the Valuation Advisory project?

1205. How clearly defined were the objectives for this Valuation Advisory project?

1206. What skills did you need that were missing on this Valuation Advisory project?

1207. How useful was the content of the training you received in preparation for the use of the product/ service?

1208. How effective were Best Practices & Lessons Learned from prior Valuation Advisory projects utilized in this Valuation Advisory project?

1209. How effective was the quality assurance process?

1210. Are there any data that you have overlooked in identifying lessons?

1211. Who had fiscal authority to manage the funding for the Valuation Advisory project, did that work?

1212. How effective was the training you received in preparation for the use of the product/service?

1213. If you had to do this Valuation Advisory project again, what is the one thing that you would change (related to process, not to technical solutions)?

1214. How timely were Progress Reports provided to the Valuation Advisory project Manager by Team Members?

1215. Was sufficient advance training conducted and/or information provided to enable the already stated affected by the changes to adjust to and accommodate them?

1216. What was helpful to know when planning the deployment?

1217. What should have been accomplished during predeployment that was not accomplished?

1218. How was the quality of products/processes assured?

1219. How effective was Valuation Advisory project Team member training?

Index

256

submit 11
submitted   11, 195
subset 20
sub-teams   206
succeed   44, 81
success   18, 32, 35, 40-43, 59-60, 62, 73, 80, 83, 86, 95, 97,
103-104, 152, 191, 197, 206, 226-227, 234
successes   81
successful   63, 76, 82, 96, 141, 191
suddenly   176
sufficient   109, 190, 213, 236
suggest   210
suggested   71, 156, 195
suitable   43, 202
summarize   144
summarized   128
supervisor   204
supplier   93, 167, 185, 229
suppliers   25, 54, 81, 200, 228-229
supplies   149, 167, 224
supply 135
support   7, 64, 74, 76-77, 92, 94, 103, 118, 139, 157, 183,
216, 222
supported   35, 55, 172
supporting   64, 76, 168
supportive   113, 165
supposed   199
surface   71
SUSTAIN   2, 67, 79
Sustaining   77, 136
symptom   17, 39
system 11-12, 57, 76, 81, 90, 118, 127, 129, 141, 164, 195, 199-
201, 216, 219
systematic   128
systems   45, 50, 52-53, 62, 75, 81, 189, 218, 225, 229
tackle 39
tactics 197-198
Taguchi   144
tailored   184
takers 122
taking 38, 191, 216
talent 89
talents 97

275

Lightning Source UK Ltd.
Milton Keynes UK
UKHW011820180219
337526UK00012B/1215/P